WOMEN'S FOOTBALL

THE HISTORY, THE STARS, THE STATS AND THE GOALS!

EVE AINSWORTH
Illustrated by Dan Leydon

GAME CHANGERS

WOMEN'S FOOTBALL
THE HISTORY, THE STARS, THE STATS AND THE GOALS!

wren
&rook

First published in Great Britain in 2022 by Wren & Rook

ISBN: 978 1 5263 6581 1
eBook ISBN: 978 1 5263 6582 8

1 3 5 7 9 10 8 6 4 2

Wren & Rook
An imprint of
Hachette Children's Group
Part of Hodder & Stoughton
Carmelite House
50 Victoria Embankment
London EC4Y 0DZ

An Hachette UK Company
www.hachette.co.uk
www.hachettechildrens.co.uk

Printed and bound in Great Britain by Clays Ltd,
Elcograf S.p.A.

The player statistics in this book were valid at the time
of going to press, however it is possible that these may
have changed since the publication of this book.

*Dedicated to the powerful and strong
women in my life – my mum, my sisters,
my nieces and my incredible daughter.*

*This is also dedicated to the many wonderful women
who have strived for better. Who have fought for their
beliefs and never given up on their dreams.*

Keep believing.

*Thank you to historian Gail Newsham for her continued
wisdom, support and expert knowledge.*

CONTENTS

INTRODUCTION
THE WARM-UP

Welcome to you all, amazing football fans! Maybe you are a football player, maybe you are a huge football fan or maybe you have only just caught up with the wonder of the Lionesses after watching their fierce, winning performance in Euro 2022. Either way, I'm pleased you are here. You're in for an exciting ride.

You might already know a lot about the game or you might discover incredible new stories and facts, but by the end of this book I hope you'll feel totally amazed by the journey women's football has taken – and how much hard work has got us here.

It's really quite amazing.

I have always loved football. As a young girl growing up, I would stand in the terraces cheering on my team. I heard a lot of prejudice ('you shouldn't be here' or 'girls know nothing about football') and a lot of people thought that football was a man's game. I didn't think to argue against it: we couldn't play football at school, there weren't any local girls' teams and women's football was never on TV. I guess I thought it was 'normal' that women didn't play football. How bad is that! Even worse, I didn't realise the MASSIVE part women had played in footballing history. I just assumed that they had never played a part at all.

It was only when I was older and researching my *Dick, Kerr Girls* book series that I realised how little I knew about the facts of women's football! Women's role in football was just as significant as men's and there were so many people who had fought behind the scenes to change the way things were, right up to the present day. Not only that – female football players had been treated shockingly by the people in charge of the game (more on that later).

Sadly, there are still misconceptions about women's football and you might hear people saying inaccurate things like:

'Oh, it's good women are playing, but they will never be good as men.'

'People aren't interested in women's football.'

'Women don't play to the same level as men.'

'Women's football is just different to men's.'

None of these things are true and – if you don't already know all about it – we're going to find out why. We're going to uncover the incredible history of the women's game, meet footballing heroes from the past and the winning team today, compare facts and figures about all your favourite players, meet some international stars and celebrate everything that is mind-blowing, goal-scoring and crowd-cheering about women's football.

You will also be able to quiz yourself (or your family and friends) and create your own dream team. Can you imagine being the next England manager? Or perhaps you see yourself as a future Lioness playing in a side that you have totally designed?

This is an exciting time to be a fan of women's football, so let's enjoy the ride through record-breaking attendances, FA bans and pioneering sportswomen. Are you ready to become a gamechanger too?

The ref's whistle is about to blow . . .

CHAPTER ONE
THE KICK-OFF

It's important that we begin at the beginning . . . And where's that, you might ask? Who kicked it all off? Which women were key to driving the game forwards? Let's travel back to the roots of women's football.

Many people think that in the UK, women's football has only been around for a relatively short time, and certainly not as long as men's football. Well, how daft are they! It's likely women have been playing football for as long as men, but unlike men, women have faced sexual discrimination, so fewer records have been kept about women's football. This makes it harder to work out *exactly* when women's football began but we DO know that some of the earliest factual reports of women playing football in the UK go back to at least as early as the seventeenth century!

And we also know that throughout history women loved playing football because it was fun and much more exciting than their normal day-to-day lives. For many, their lives were hard work – so sport was a release and a way of making friends. It was a social event! Many early pioneers were determined to play as much of the game as they could. We can travel back quite far in history to meet our earliest footballing stars . . .

EARLY PIONEERS: ROYALS AND FISHERWOMAN

- One of the earliest footballing accounts suggests that in June 1568, somewhere between Carlisle Castle and the Scottish border, Mary Queen of Scots witnessed a football match between members of her entourage. The game was said to have lasted for two hours!

- In Scotland, as early as 1628 there were reports of football being played by both men and women, and 'folk football' was part of villager celebrations during fairs or holidays.

- There's also a report about a group of fisherwoman footballers, known as the Fisherrow Fishwives, who played in Musselburgh, Scotland from around 1795. These women (some as young as fourteen) worked very long hours selling their wares. It was hard work for little pay and the women often walked for miles between towns carrying heavy baskets of fish. To stay strong, the women played sports and they also sang in choirs because community was important to them. Friendly football matches helped them to keep fit and brought everyone together, so it's not surprising they liked a kick-about!

'Well, it's a lovely bright Shrove Tuesday afternoon so the Fisherrow Fishwives are out in force today for a match that should bring interest far and wide. Now, am I right in thinking that this game is usually a friendly between the married and unmarried women?'

'Yes, that's right, and interestingly it's usually the married women who win.'

'Any idea why?'

'No one quite knows, but strap yourself in - this should be an interesting game.'

VICTORIAN VISIONARIES

Women's football didn't really pop up in the history books again until the late nineteenth century. In these days, middle-class young girls were beginning to play competitive sports (such as hockey) in school - although girls received less education than boys, were barred from university and if they were not wealthy, they could expect to work in very low-paid jobs.

At the same time, in 1863, Association Football was set up to create more official games and lay out the rules of the game. Fast forward to 1881 and the first women's football match (using these new Association Football rules) was played in Scotland. Teams representing England and Scotland were going to battle it out and the local press reported the excitement. On the day, around 1,000 people came to watch and Scotland won 3-0. That wasn't the end - the following week they played again - but this time the crowd had increased to 5,000! According to newspaper reports, the second game was disappointing and the crowd invaded the pitch and began to riot. Unfortunately, this meant that the planned third match was cancelled, and women's football took a bit of a knocking.

Slightly later (around 1894–1895) in England, a young woman aptly named Nettie Honeyball decided she'd start a ladies' football team, so she placed a newspaper advertisement in the *Morning Leader*. Nettie wanted women to be able to make money from the game, the same way men could. Around thirty women saw her advert and signed up to play, and the British Ladies' team began! Nettie even managed to persuade some of the leading male coaches of the day to train them.

Not much is known about Nettie except that she was between twenty-five and thirty years old and believed that women should be able to enjoy the same sports as men. She wanted the club to show the world that women were not 'ornamental' creatures. Her team would attract the finest female footballers, so when she advertised for players, Nettie announced that the women would play:

> *'A manly game and show that it could be womanly as well.'*

In March 1895 the first British Ladies' match took place at Nightingale Lane, watched by over 10,000 spectators. This was a great number for the day and the match was between London and the surrounding areas: effectively North London vs South London. The players wore blouses, knickerbockers fastened below the knee and caps on their heads. It was sponsored by the Club President, Lady Florence Dixie, who was also a war reporter for the London Morning Post and a skilled horsewoman.

The match ended up being a 7-1 victory for the North and many more fixtures were arranged by Lady Dixie. The women played many games throughout England, Scotland and Northern Ireland.

Although it was popular, many people were outraged and the *British Medical Journal* published an article claiming that football could expose women to 'violence' and damage their organs! One journalist writing for the *Manchester Guardian* said of the match:

'When the novelty has worn off, I do not think that women's football will attract the crowds.'

Although the British Ladies' team went on to play many games, they continued to face lots of criticism. Sadly, a lack of finances and support meant that the club folded a few years later and they slipped into the history books. Women's football would go quiet for a little while. That was until the start of a life-changing event. The First World War was about to begin.

You Wouldn't Believe It

YWBI

'So was Nettie Honeyball actually her real name?'

'Well, some people think that she might have made it up as a pseudonym. It's fun though, isn't it?'

'It is a great name, but why would she have made it up?'

'Well, lots of people would have been against her at the time – they wouldn't have liked a lady of her standing to have been involved in football.'

'Well, if that's true then who was the real Nettie Honeyball? Do we know?'

'No one is sure, but she might have been Jesse Mary Ann Smith, a middle-class lady and the sister-in-law of Alfred Hewitt Smith, who was the British Ladies' manager. Bit of a coincidence . . .'

'Well, whoever she was, she was pretty important to football, wasn't she?'

'She really was. She was an incredible early influence on women's football and, if it was a pseudonym, what a great name to have chosen!'

PLAY ON, DICK, KERR GIRLS

In 1914 the Great War began in Europe and it changed life for everyone. England needed a lot of things when war broke out. It needed soldiers. It needed weapons and it needed people to help produce them. Because of this, England also needed women!

'Your country needs you' posters were stuck up in every town and city asking women to help with the war effort by working as nurses, or in factories, or on the railways and farms. Many extra workers were needed to fill the jobs that had belonged to men who had left to fight.

One particular factory in the north-west of England was looking for munition workers. The Dick, Kerr factory had previously made electronic goods for the local tramway - but now it was producing ammunition for the war. As the workers headed to war, the factory needed young, strong women to take up the work. It was grim work, because the women were handling explosives and many lost fingers, noses or eyes. Similar to our fishwives in the eighteenth century, these women quickly became a strong team, and their friendships and tough willpower helped them through the hard work.

The women working in these factories were also encouraged to exercise and enjoy their lunch breaks, because fit and healthy workers would be more productive! Many of the girls played football, as it was a game they had learnt in the streets where they lived. Since the turn of the century, football had become more of a working-class sport, and for families in the poorest areas, it was a fun way to bring everyone together. So it was here, in the yard of the Dick, Kerr factory, that another twist on the women's football journey was about to begin . . .

In October 1917 a young worker named Grace Sibbert was teasing the young lads who were still working at the factory. Grace was one of the young women who liked kicking a ball about on her break, and she had heard that these lads had not been playing well in their local football games. Grace, perhaps feeling a bit mischievous, had apparently said, 'Call yourself a football team? We could do better than you lot!'

The boys, not liking this at all, challenged Grace to a game, which she accepted, saying, 'Come on, girls, let's give it a go. It'll be a laugh.' She assembled a team of fellow female players to compete against the boys on a field in Preston. Sadly, there is no record of the result, but word of the match caught on. A matron of the local Moor Park Hospital, where injured soldiers were treated, approached the Dick, Kerr factory to see if the girls would be interested in playing a charity match to raise funds. Not long after, a clerk at the factory, named Alfred Franklin, saw the talent in the Dick, Kerr girls and the potential to raise much-needed money for charity – so he agreed to manage them. The Dick, Kerr Ladies were born.

On Christmas Day 1917 the Dick, Kerr Ladies played the neighbouring Arundel Coulthard Foundry. The girls could hardly believe their eyes when over 10,000 spectators arrived to see them play! The Dick, Kerr Ladies won the match in commanding fashion, 4-0, and raised approximately £600 (that's equivalent to more than £29,000 now).

This was the beginning of an amazing period for women's football, which saw the Dick, Kerr Ladies attract large crowds, go on international tours, become celebrities and raise the equivalent of *millions* of pounds' worth of money for charity. They were the Lionesses of their time, commanding respect wherever they played and defying the many critics who still believed that women should not be playing football.

It was an exciting time. It really did seem that women's football was on the march – and nothing could stop it. But the best was yet to come . . .

You Wouldn't Believe It

'Now here's a fact for you: did you know that the women who worked in the munitions factories during the war were nicknamed the Canaries. Any idea why?'

'I'm guessing it's nothing to do with Norwich Town FC?'

'Afraid not. It was because the chemicals they were working with turned their skin a nasty shade of yellow, but luckily it was only a temporary side effect.'

'It certainly doesn't sound like the best way to stand out on a pitch.'

GOAL-SCORING IN GOODISON PARK

By the end of the First World War the Dick, Kerr Ladies were becoming a big name in the footballing world. They had established themselves as a skilful team and crowds were keen to see what all the fuss was about. The Dick, Kerr Ladies fans grew and grew. Who couldn't help but fall in love with a talented team that worked hard together, never gave up, barely lost a game and raised loads of money for charity?

You Wouldn't Believe It

'Here we are on 16 December 1920, and I think we are going to be watching a memorable charity match tonight.'

'Well, I'm always excited to see the Dick, Kerr girls play, but I'm surprised we are here so late in the day. It's nearly dark!'

'That's why this is a memorable game - see those searchlights over there? The Dick, Kerr girls have borrowed anti-aircraft searchlights from the War Office to light up the pitch tonight. This is the first time floodlights have been used in such a way. They've even painted the ball white so it can be spotted in every corner.'

'I think the crowd will be impressed with that.'

'Yes, just look at the numbers here tonight. We've got over 10,000 in the crowd to watch the Dick, Kerr girls light up the country in more ways than one.'

'Surely this is one for the history books?'

The women also had the fortune to play internationally in France, a country where women's football was developing quickly, so their reputation was growing at home and abroad. The hype was building that this team was as good as any men's side!

Perhaps one of the most exciting events to happen in women's football occurred on Boxing Day in 1920 when the Dick, Kerr manager, Alfred Franklin, decided to arrange a match that would defy expectations. The match would be played at Goodison Park, one of the biggest grounds in the country, and the hope was that the team would be able to raise even *more* money for charity than ever before.

Remember that only a few years before this, women's football was seen as a bit of a silly novelty – so just the idea of having the Dick, Kerr Ladies play on a major footballing ground (and a men's one) was a big step! The Dick, Kerr Ladies were to play St Helens, another exciting ladies' team based in Merseyside. The teams hoped that many fans would want to come and see these talented women play . . .

All expectations were blown out of the water when over **53,000** spectators tried to pack themselves into the ground. It was a squeeze, and even then, 10,000–14,000 people were unable to get inside. Many of them hung around, standing in the surrounding streets, hoping to pick up on what was going on from outside the ground. This wasn't a game they wanted to miss! The match was a huge national event with lots of press attention. The attendance remains the biggest in English women's domestic football - and was the biggest English international record for 92 years (until Team GB beat Brazil in the 2012 Olympics in front of 70,584 fans).

The crowd was so excited that the teams had to have a police escort take them safely into their changing rooms. Only years before, women's football was barely spoken about, and now our footballers were being treated like celebrities! They were loved because they were so exciting to watch and they made the game a truly uplifting experience.

So when the game started, they ran out to roaring crowds, and the Dick, Kerr Ladies played their hearts out. They won by an impressive 4-0 and raised £3,115 for charity, which is the equivalent of around £100,000 in today's money. The size of the crowd was proof, if any was needed, that women's football was *just* as popular as men's, that people wanted to see women play and that female footballers were just as talented as their male counterparts. And the Dick, Kerr Ladies were not alone. There were other teams popping up around the country, all keen to prove that they had the skills to succeed.

Surely the only way was up? The future seemed bright for our fantastic footballers. But waiting on the sidelines were some shadowy characters who didn't like what was happening in football at all. In fact, they were keen to bring an end to it as fast as they could.

But would they have their way? You will find out very soon . . .

AWAY GAMES GO GLOBAL

Women's football was taking off beyond the domestic matches too. On Boxing Day in 1917 teams representing England and Ireland faced each other in Belfast, Ireland (now called Northern Ireland). This is thought to be the earliest international women's match, played by women who all worked in munitions factories, much like the Dick, Kerr Ladies. This game was probably arranged as a sort of 'exhibition match' to show off what the players were capable of. It was reported that over 20,000 spectators came to watch the match and the result was a 4-1 victory to the English team. But we don't know much else – possibly because the FA didn't formally recognise it as a proper football match, so there weren't many reports about it . . . But we do know that it was a game that drew in the crowds and had a lot of interest at the time.

'Have you heard of Bill McCracken?'

'No, who is he?'

'Well, Bill McCracken was a famous footballer, manager and scout in the 1920s world of football, and he also probably organised the early international match between England and Ireland. He was a big supporter of the women's game and raised lots of money for charity too.'

'He sounds like a memorable guy.'

'Not only that, but McCracken is also credited with inventing the offside trap, which at the time forced the opposition to break the offside rule. He was so successful at it, the rules of the game had to be adjusted!'

'Well, folks, that's definitely a name to remember!'

Back to the Dick, Kerr girls: by 1920, the team were making waves in Europe as the first women's football team to tour another country. They had already invited a French team to tour around England with them and then they travelled to France to take part in the second leg. In France they played to large crowds of around 14,000–22,000 (a BIG crowd at the time) and they won two and drew one of their matches. Many men and ex-service men were in the crowds to cheer on the girls' impressive play. This was the start of many tours between the two teams and also the beginning of Dick, Kerr's international football. This wasn't their last trip: they would go on to play in Canada and America, bringing in more fans and more attention.

However, the first ever **official** women's international match wasn't held until April 1971 and was between France and the Netherlands. A year later, the first women's international match in Great Britain was held in Scotland, when England beat Scotland 3–2.

So why was there such a gap between the Boxing Day match of 1920 and the officially recognised international matches in the 1970s? A gap of over fifty years!

For the answer to that question, we need to move on to the bumpiest part of the women's football's journey yet – and quite possibly the most shocking of all . . .

THE BAN AND THE FOOTBALLING REBELS

By 1921 women's football was on the rise. Teams like the Dick, Kerr Ladies were drawing in huge crowds. New teams were being formed up and down the country. Many more factory workers were forming teams alongside those working in other places like tearooms. The war had ended, but many women were still working and enjoying playing football in their downtime. Although a lot of the women's teams were set up to raise money for charity, it was clear that many of the women liked the competitive nature too. They wanted to succeed, and they wanted to win!

Lots of other changes were happening at this time too: in 1919 Nancy Astor became the first woman to take up her elected seat in the House of Commons (the first woman to be elected, Constance Markievicz, won a seat in 1918 but didn't take it in political protest). In the same year, 1918, women were awarded the right to vote. However, not ALL women could vote. They had to be over thirty and meet a property requirement, so this only included about two-thirds of women at the time. There was a long way to go, but this was a huge step in women's equal rights history after many, many years of campaigning. Women would finally be able to vote equally to men in 1928.

With plenty of changes going on, not everybody was happy about the speed of progression. Complaints had been made to newspapers and to the FA that women should not be playing football. It was seen as unladylike and bad for their health. Clearly rattled by these views, the FA sought medical opinions and were told by many doctors that football *could* be a dangerous sport for women. These same doctors seemed unable to explain why other sports, such as hockey, weren't deemed as dangerous, but perhaps they were viewed as being more 'ladylike'.

On 5 December the FA held a crucial meeting. They discussed the medical reports that had been presented to them, both for and against women playing football. It's also fair to assume that they considered the popular success of teams like the Dick, Kerr Ladies. That's why it's so shocking that by the end of the meeting the FA decided to **ban** women's football from taking place on any of their grounds. It was a unanimous decision and quite possibly one of the most damaging acts to be carried out in British sporting history. Many believe that the decision was made to stop women's football becoming more popular than men's, and although this has never been proven, it's difficult to understand why the board chose to make

this decision.

Daily News

WOMEN'S FOOTBALL OFFICIALLY BANNED

Just as it was beginning to soar, women's football had its wings clipped. The ban would stay in place for 50 years! Now you know why the English women's team couldn't play an international match until 1972. And things were going to become *very* difficult for our female footballers during those 50 years.

But this didn't stop them.

The Dick, Kerr Ladies vowed to continue playing, although their games would now be on local pitches, not the likes of Goodison Park. They still managed to attract crowds, albeit much smaller ones, made up of fans who were determined that women's football shouldn't be allowed to die - but many other fans drifted away, frustrated that they could no longer watch their favourite players perform in the stadiums. Meanwhile, new footballers were pushing themselves forward, like Lily Parr, Chris McCoy, Wendy Owen and Elaine Badcock and we will discover the incredible stories of these players later on.

Women's football had been served a terrible injustice. An injustice that remained for half a century and held back promising and talented sportspeople. But our women weren't going to give up. The fight back had only just begun!

You Wouldn't Believe It YWBI

'I can't believe that the FA ban on women's football stayed in place for 50 years?!'

'Can you imagine if that were to happen to our Lionesses now?'

'And can you imagine if it had happened to the men's team of the time?'

'It would have put men's football back as well, wouldn't it?'

'It certainly would have done ... That's why, even though the decision was accepted in 1921, we must never forget the original Lionesses who didn't stop roaring. They fought hard to put women's football back where it belonged: on the same level as men's football.'

WOMEN'S FOOTBALL RISES AGAIN

For a time, women's football was out of the spotlight. Teams still existed, but they had to play on park fields instead of professional pitches. Many skilled footballers had to make do, playing on the streets and enjoying the game as best they could. Frustrated by the fact that they would never be seen as professional footballers, no matter how good they were.

Although the ban was still in place by the 1960s, the FA's attitude had been slowly changing - they were starting to think that maybe football wasn't so unsuitable for women after all. In 1969 the Women's FA (WFA) was formed and by 1971 the FA ban was finally lifted. A year later England would have their first team competing internationally.

However, things were still moving as slow as a winger with lead in their boots!

In 1994 the FA took over WFA's national league and set up a Premier League with three established divisions. By

2001 they agreed that football was a key sport for women to take part in, both at school and after. Now the game was gaining momentum and in 2005 England hosted the UEFA Women's Championship. Although England went out in the group stages, the buzz around the team was growing. Was women's football on the rise again?

It certainly seemed so, because England qualified for the 2007 FIFA World Cup in China and hopes were high. They went on to reach the quarter-finals, losing out to an impressive USA side. Excitement was also building domestically, as Arsenal, a fearsome and growing team, became the first British team to win the UEFA Women's Cup – one of the top prizes in Europe.

With domestic clubs doing so well, the England team looking stronger than ever and talk of a women's super league about to be set up, it's no wonder everyone was feeling very excited.

It's mind-boggling to think that the game was banned for 50 years and truly amazing to think about the people who kept fighting against the ban. We're about to meet some of those world-changing players, who never gave up despite the odds . . .

You Wouldn't Believe It YWBI

'Here we are, live at the opening 2005 Women's Championship match in England. What an atmosphere already!'

'I know, I can't quite believe it - how many fans are here?'

'Over 29,000 fans! That's quite the crowd! And that's just those who are here with us today - there are more than 2.9 million tuned in at home watching it live.'

'That's amazing. The crowd really are ready!'

CHAPTER TWO
THE ORIGINAL LIONESSES

Are you ready to meet some of the amazing players – from the past and recent times – who helped get our game to where it is now? These are the original Lionesses, if you like, and they've got goal-scoring stories to tell . . .

LILY PARR

Lily Parr was probably one of the earliest superstar footballers. So, who was she and what made her so special? So special, in fact, that she now has a statue in the National Football Museum!

To begin with, Parr was known for being a deadly striker with a lethal shot, and she was seen as being better than many male players of the time.

Parr was just fifteen years old when she joined the Dick, Kerr Ladies in 1920 and was said to be very shy. She didn't like too much attention on her, but it was hard for people to ignore her naturally gifted play. After the FA ban in 1921, Parr continued to play for the

Facts & Stats
Lily Parr

- Born: 1905
- Position: Left winger
- Club(s): St Helens Ladies, Dick, Kerr Ladies, Preston Ladies
- Goals: over 900
- Super Skill: Lethal left foot
- Fantastic Fact: It was reported that when Parr was in her early twenties and was practising shots against a male goalkeeper, he challenged her to take the most powerful shot she had against him. So she did . . . She supposedly nearly broke the poor goalie's arm!

Dick, Kerr Ladies and scored an incredible total of over 900 goals in her 30-year playing career! That is some record. She played internationally and encouraged other girls and women to take up the game.

She is now recognised as one of the greatest players of all time and she was the first woman to be inducted into the National Football Museum's Hall of Fame in 2002.

What a hero!

CHRIS MCCOY

This legendary footballer vowed to keep playing football despite the ban.

Chris McCoy started playing football when she was five years old. She was well known for her fearless tackles and amazing pace on the left wing. By the age of thirteen she was being compared to George Best, who was a legendary 1960s footballer at the time. Because of her impressive skills, McCoy was invited to take part in trials in

Manchester. The problem was that in the early 1960s, the football ban was still in place, so despite McCoy being the best player at the trial, she couldn't be signed. One scout admitted that if she had been a boy she would've been signed immediately. Many people might have been defeated by that, but not Chris McCoy. She vowed to play astonishing football anyway, but she did always wonder what might have been, if she'd be allowed to play professionally all those years ago . . .

PATRICIA GREGORY

It wasn't just incredible players who were influential in the early days. Young football fans could also change history, like this one . . .

In 1967 nineteen-year-old Patricia Gregory was with her dad watching Tottenham win the FA Cup. Although she really enjoyed the game, she couldn't help but feel frustrated by the end of it and asked her dad why girls couldn't play football too. It just didn't seem fair.

Unaware of the FA ban, Gregory angrily wrote a letter to her local newspaper complaining about the lack of opportunities for female players. When her letter was published in the paper, girls wrote to Gregory asking if they could join her team. Well, Gregory didn't have a team, so she decided it was about time she started one! At first the council wouldn't let her hire a pitch, so Gregory wrote to the press again, and this time a football magazine and another men's team told her she could use their pitches. Gregory's team, White Ribbon, was born.

That's not all: Gregory's letters were seen by Arthur Hobbs, who was already running tournaments for female footballers. Together Gregory and Hobbs helped create the South East of England League. During the next two years (1967-1969) they would set up leagues and together form the base of the Women's Football Association (WFA). Just two years later, the FA ban would be lifted.

It's incredible to think that one frustrated football fan, who decided to write a letter, was in the right place at the right time to go on and play a big role in establishing the women's football league that is still in place today. Her determination and hard work, along with the help of others, have changed footballing history!

So what about the young footballers who were playing just as the FA ban was lifted. How did that affect their game?

ELAINE BADCOCK

Elaine Badcock often played football with the boys in her school, even though she wasn't allowed to play in the school team.

This was really frustrating as she knew she was just as good – if not better – than most of the boys. She later played for local women's teams such as Chester Ladies, then after the ban was lifted in 1971, she was selected to be part of the English side in 1976.

It was amazing to be able to play officially! However, it was tricky to get an England team together because the players weren't paid, so they had to juggle full-time jobs and couldn't necessarily afford to take time off to play or to travel to matches. The team also had to raise money to pay for basic things and they shared only one full team's kit, which they had to quickly wash when they had back-to-back games.

Badcock juggled her full-time work with her football fixtures and training, and her resilience, her love of the game and the excitement of playing helped her keep going.

WENDY OWEN

In 1972, when she was only eighteen, Wendy Owen became another star in the original England squad.

Owen played for England between 1972 and 1977, but that's not all – she was capped 16 times and played matches across Europe. Owen had been inspired by the England men's 1966 World Cup heroes and dreamed of having a similar career. She was training to be a PE teacher when she trialled for the new women's football squad, and when she was accepted into the team, she told her teacher training college that she would need some time off to play for the squad. They didn't take her footballing ambitions seriously – and it's fair to say this spurred Owen on even more!

Owen was a talented and ambitious centre-half, who was determined to show the country that women's footballers should be judged by their skill and ability, and she has since gone on to write a book about her footballing career.

Now let's hear the stories of some of the finest footballers of recent times, starting with Fara Williams.

FARA WILLIAMS

Fara Williams is one of the most capped England players of all time!

Williams made 172 appearances, featured in three World Cups and helped the Lionesses achieve the runner-up spot in Euro 2009. At domestic level, Williams won two Women's Super League titles with Liverpool and the FA Cup with Arsenal and Everton.

Facts & Stats

Fara Williams

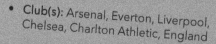

- Born: 1984

- Position: Midfielder

- Club(s): Arsenal, Everton, Liverpool, Chelsea, Charlton Athletic, England

- Senior Caps: 172

- Super Skill: Set piece specialist

- Fantastic Fact: Aged twelve, Williams nearly missed her trial at Chelsea after getting on the wrong bus. She had to walk for over an hour and arrived just half an hour before the end. She must have been very impressive in the small time she had, because she was selected – and her professional football dreams began!

Williams' journey into football wasn't the easiest one. She started playing at the age of seven and this focus, and the people she met, changed her life when she became homeless as a teenager. Her Everton and England coaches helped her get into a homeless hostel and get the support she needed.

She kept playing football and built an incredible career. Williams was a naturally skilful midfielder: she scored in the Euro 2009 tournament (when the team reached the final before being beaten by Germany), and she was also the top scorer in the 2011 World Cup qualifiers. She didn't stop there – she scored the decisive penalty in the 2015 World Cup in Canada, securing a third-place spot for England and landing them a victory against Germany.

Williams overcame the odds in her life, as well as on the pitch, and achieved many of her football dreams.

STEPH HOUGHTON MBE

Steph Houghton used to go to football camps at Sunderland FC in her school holidays, which is where she was spotted by a football scout, and her glittering footballing career began.

Houghton's dad was a semi-professional footballer and although she excelled at several sports, it was clear that football was her strongest. She played at left-back and centre defence and became a consistent defender.

She signed for Leeds United in 2007 and was named FA Women's Young Player of the Year in 2008. Two years later, she won the FA Cup with Leeds and then signed to Arsenal, where once again she would go on to lift the FA Cup.

She didn't stop there – Houghton has represented England over 100 times! Although she has been hit hard by injuries, she has managed to make full recoveries and continue playing, even going on to

Facts & Stats
Steph Houghton MBE

- Born: 1988
- Position: Defender
- Club(s): Sunderland, Leeds United, Arsenal, Manchester City, England
- Senior Goals: 13
- Senior Caps: 121
- Super Skill: Leadership
- Fantastic Fact: Houghton was involved in the 2019 World Cup semi-final against the USA when she famously missed a penalty in the shoot-out. She did not let this disappointment affect her for too long and used the experience to help drive her on even further.

wear the captain's armband. She signed for Manchester City in 2014 and became a key member of their team. She was also the first female footballer to appear on the front cover of *Shoot* magazine.

All in all, Houghton has won four Continental Cups, three FA Cups and the FA Women's Super League with Manchester City. She led the England football team to a bronze medal in the 2015 World Cup, represented Team GB at the Olympic Games and has been named Manchester City's Player of the Year twice. She was unlucky to miss the 2022 Euro campaign because of an injury.

In 2016 Houghton was awarded an MBE for her achievements both on and off the pitch. Although she struggles with injuries, she's still playing football, and her long-term goal is to inspire the next generation of girls to play football.

KELLY SMITH MBE

Kelly Smith is one of England's greatest ever forwards...

Smith was spotted at a young age, playing as a teenager for Wembley before being picked for Arsenal. Smith had already been asked to leave two boys' teams for being too good! Smith enjoyed a great first season with Arsenal and helped them to win the title over Liverpool, but, keen to develop her skills further, she moved to the USA. She played for the New Jersey Lady Stallions, but unfortunately injury affected her early career in America.

During this time, she was still playing for England when she was fit.

Facts & Stats
Kelly Smith MBE

- **Born:** 1978
- **Position:** Forward
- **Club(s):** Wembley, Arsenal, New Jersey Lady Stallions, Philadelphia Charge, New Jersey Wild Cats, Boston Breakers
- **Senior Goals:** 46
- **Senior Caps:** 117
- **Super Skill:** Super shooting
- **Fantastic Fact:** Smith now works with the FA Girls' Football School Partnership to help encourage women's football in schools and after-school clubs. She hopes that more girls will get the opportunity to play the game!

Smith was a uniquely talented player with a clinical shot, excellent passing skills and lightning pace, and in 2004 she returned to Arsenal. The following season she was the Women's Premier League top scorer and was a huge part of Arsenal's quadruple-winning campaign. She was unstoppable and scored 30 goals in 34 games! Smith really was regarded as a world-class striker now. Smith moved back to the USA again and played for the Boston Breakers briefly before returning to her beloved Arsenal, where she coached as well as playing.

Smith was also a key player for England. Aged only seventeen, she scored her first international goal. This was the start of an amazing run where she went on to score 45 goals for England in 20 years. Only male players such as Lineker, Charlton and Rooney have scored more goals for England.

RACHEL YANKEY OBE

Rachel Yankey was an extremely talented winger and one of the first female footballers to be given a professional footballing contract by the FA.

Aged just seventeen, Yankey was playing for Arsenal and had achieved her first England cap. She was able to help Arsenal win the Premier League and two cup doubles in 1998 and 1999. Then in 2000 she signed the first ever women's professional contract with Fulham and

Facts & Stats
Rachel Yankey OBE

- **Born:** 1979
- **Position:** Forward/winger
- **Club(s):** Arsenal, Laval Dynamites, Fulham, Birmingham City, New Jersey Wildcats, Notts County
- **Senior Goals:** 19
- **Senior Caps:** 129
- **Super Skill:** Fast feet and deadly finishing
- **Fantastic Fact:** When Yankey was just eight years old, she asked her hairdresser to shave all her hair off. This wasn't for fashionable reasons; rather, she wanted to play football as a boy and not be judged, so she called herself 'Ray' and played in disguise.

played a huge part in their treble-winning performance in 2002.

Yankey played briefly for Birmingham and a spell in the USA before returning to Arsenal, where she remained for 11 years. She was a goal machine! She averaged a goal every three games, usually from a wide position. In all, she won five Premier League medals, was involved in seven FA Women's Cups and two Premier League Cup wins, and was a key player in the club's 2007 UEFA campaign.

For England, Yankey achieved 129 caps and 19 goals and was instrumental in the Euro 2005 campaign. She remains one of the most capped players in England's history – and she remains a Lioness legend!

ALEX SCOTT MBE

Do you know this famous footballer from the TV? Now a sports presenter, Alex Scott is a legendary Lioness too.

Scott developed her skills in Arsenal's youth academy and soon became known as one of the greatest attacking right-backs. Scott was a key player in Arsenal's double-winning side in 2005/2006 and would help the club to secure the title, the FA Cup and Premier League Cup the following season.

Facts & Stats
Alex Scott

- Born: 1984
- Position: Defender
- Club(s): Arsenal, Birmingham City, Boston Breakers
- Senior Goals: 12
- Senior Caps: 140
- Super Skill: Composure
- Fantastic Fact: Scott is now a leading TV broadcaster and commentator on BBC and Sky Sports and one of the most recognised female footballers of all time.

Scott was also instrumental in helping Arsenal win the UEFA Championship, scoring a last-minute goal against the Swedish favourites. This win meant that Scott was one of the first players to have won the quadruple in England. How amazing is that?!

After another double-winning performance in 2007/2008, Scott moved to the USA and played for the Boston Breakers for two years, before returning to her beloved Arsenal to see out her career – where she would help the Gunners retain their Women's Super League title and in 2016 helped take them to the final of the FA Cup where they beat Chelsea 1-0.

Scott was an integral member of the England team after making her debut in 2004. She played in four UEFA Euro tournaments and three World Cups – eventually making 140 appearances and scoring 12 goals.

CASEY STONEY

One of the most influential of England's players, Casey Stoney was a player, captain and manager.

A gifted defender, Stoney was playing for Chelsea aged just twelve, but was soon spotted by Arsenal, who she joined in 1999 aged seventeen. Just a year later, Stoney was making her England debut against France.

Stoney was part of the 2000/2001 Arsenal side that won the treble and then she moved on to Charlton to further develop her career. It was here where Stoney, as captain, led the club to their first ever FA Cup final in 2001! Then, in 2004, she helped them secure the FA Premier League and, a year later the FA Cup too.

Sadly, Charlton had to disband their women's team in 2007 following the relegation of the men's team from the Premier League, so Stoney returned to Chelsea. After two years, she became interim player–manager at only twenty-seven years old, and she was awarded the 2008 FA International Player of the Year for her achievements.

Internationally, Stoney helped England to reach the final of Euro 2009 and she was instrumental in all four of England's games in the 2011 World Cup. Months after this she became captain and led Team GB to the quarter-finals at the Olympic Games.

Facts & Stats
Casey Stoney

- Born: 1982

- Position: Defender

- Club(s): Arsenal, Charlton, Chelsea, Liverpool, England

- Senior Goals: 6

- Senior Caps: 130

- Super Skill: Strength

- Fantastic Fact: Until the age of eleven, Stoney had played for boys' teams. She felt that the experience helped her learn faster and toughen up her play. She said she was heckled more by parents on the sidelines than by the players. Some of the parents didn't like to see their boys tackled by a girl!

Stoney would eventually end up playing back at Arsenal and helping them to win the FA Cup in 2014 and 2016, along with the Women's Super League Cup in 2015. She ended her playing career at Liverpool before briefly joining Phil Neville's England coaching staff in 2018 and then moving on to manage Manchester United later that same year. Stoney is now seen as one of the leading managers and has recently moved to America to become the **head coach** for San Diego Wave.

CHAPTER THREE
FOOTBALL RISES AGAIN

Now you've met some of the most impressive original Lionesses, let's dive back into the game. It's 2009 and we're about to begin the UEFA Euro final . . .

LIONESSES NEARLY OVER THE LINE

The England team were looking strong ahead of the Euros. Could this be the year that they would defy the critics and show the rest of Europe what they were capable of? As they flew out to Finland, hope was growing . . . England had a strong young side and players like Jill Scott, Karen Carney and Kelly Smith were already commanding the game domestically. Plus, with a leading manager like Hope Powell, things were looking good.

In the group stages England had a rocky start, losing 2-1 to Italy. They soon turned things around, winning against Russia and drawing against Sweden, which was just enough to put them in the quarter-finals. In the quarter-finals, England fought hard to win 3-2 against Finland and they went storming into the semi-final against the Netherlands.

In the semis England dominated with 20 shots on target to the Netherlands' five. Smith scored in the 61st minute, only for the Netherlands to equalise a few minutes later. Then, in extra-time, England's Scott landed another goal, taking the score to 2-1. The team would be facing Germany next, and the pressure and expectations were really building.

The final was a tough one and Germany put England under pressure early on by scoring in the 20th and 22nd minutes. Despite being 2-0 down, England fought on and Carney scored in the 24th minute. The game was relentless, with Germany piling on more pressure straight after half-time, and they scored another goal in the 51st minute. Smith soon gained one back with an amazing goal for England that brought the score to 3-2.

Sadly for England, Germany's dominance was clear and within minutes they scored again, before clearing up in the 73rd and 76th minutes. The final score was 6-2 to Germany. This was obviously hugely disappointing for England. It had been a huge achievement to make the final, and the team's grit and determination were proof that they had the resilience and skills to make future progress.

Meanwhile, over in Belarus, the under-19's were also taking part in the UEFA European Championship. In this final the women won 2-0 in magnificent style. Even more excitingly, a new crop of players was beginning to shine in the spotlight - Lucy Bronze, Jade Moore and Demi Stokes. These were all players who would soon end up as part of the senior squad and make names for themselves.

'Here's another football fact for you – did you know that when the England senior team reached the UEFA Championship final, it was for the first time in 25 years?!'

'That's a huge achievement and surely proof that women's football was rising up again?'

'Exactly, and remember that only 38 years before, women's football had been completely banned. Who could have thought they would reach the heady heights of a European final twice after such a long ban? There really is no stopping these Lionesses, is there?!'

'It really is amazing. I'm excited to see where they will take us next . . .'

GOING PROFESSIONAL

Nowadays the FA runs the Women's Super League (WSL), which is the highest tier of women's football in England and is made up of 12 teams. The WSL was introduced in

2011 to replace the Women's Premier League National Division, which had been the highest level of women's football and only took place during summer months.

Sixteen teams originally applied to be part of the WSL, and only eight were selected: Arsenal, Birmingham City, Bristol Academy, Chelsea, Doncaster Rovers Belles, Everton, Lincoln and Liverpool. The team that finishes top of the WSL wins the championship, but both first and second spots qualify for the UEFA Women's Champions League the following season.

In 2014 a second division was formed, and two years later it was decided that teams from the lower leagues could earn promotion to the second WSL division. This meant there was a full route between lower leagues and the WSL - and not only that, WSL would also now run in both the winter and summer seasons, like men's football.

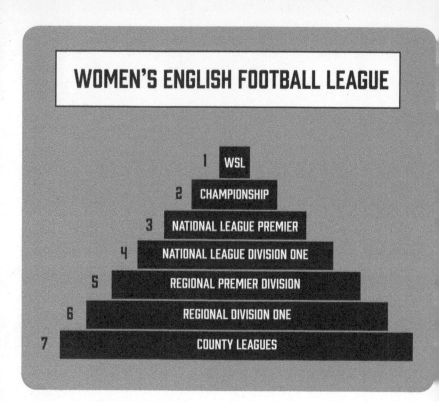

WOMEN'S ENGLISH FOOTBALL LEAGUE

1 WSL
2 CHAMPIONSHIP
3 NATIONAL LEAGUE PREMIER
4 NATIONAL LEAGUE DIVISION ONE
5 REGIONAL PREMIER DIVISION
6 REGIONAL DIVISION ONE
7 COUNTY LEAGUES

By the 2018/2019 season the WSL had become fully professional and was now called the FA Women's Super League. The professional status meant that clubs had to reapply to be included, have youth academies as part of their set up and offer players minimum hourly contracts. This was brilliant news as it meant that female footballers at the top of their game were starting to get some of the same benefits as their male counterparts (although at a much lower level).

In March 2019 Barclays were announced as title partner of the FA WSL, in what is believed to be the biggest-ever investment in the women's sport by a brand. And in 2021 another big change was announced: broadcasting companies Sky Sports and BBC agreed a deal with the FA. Now more live women's football would be broadcast on TV than ever before!

The WSL had made a clear path for women's football in England and given it professional status. With sponsorship and TV deals, there was more money in the game, and that meant more opportunities. And with the FA now fully supporting our female footballing heroes, there were more chances than ever before.

You Wouldn't Believe It YWBI

'Did you know that in 2012 Arsenal won their ninth straight title and then scored back-to-back doubles as they beat Birmingham in the Continental Cup Final?'

'No, I didn't know that. Go, Gunners!'

SHE SHOOTS, SHE SCORES

Here are some of the big moments that led up to the amazing Euro 2022 campaign.

2011 The England team reached the quarter-finals of the FIFA Women's World Cup in Germany before going out to France on penalties.

2012 Team GB reached the quarter-finals of the London Olympics, cheered on by an enthusiastic home crowd, but a strong Canadian side beat them 2-0.

2013 England were able to win the Cyprus Cup for the second time but sadly were unable to make it beyond the group stage at the European Championship finals. Hope remained strong – surely the Lionesses' time would come soon?

2014 England were able to play their first match at the new Wembley Stadium, which was a huge event, with a record crowd of 45,619 for their match against Germany. Star player Fara Williams also set a new England appearance record when she helped the Lionesses beat Sweden 4-0 in Hartlepool on her record-breaking 130th cap.

2015 The FIFA World Cup in Canada was an opportunity for the Lionesses to show that women's football was one of the most exciting sports to watch. After the Lionesses won bronze, more young fans throughout the country were paying attention to the game, signing up at local clubs and starting to believe that they could be future football stars . . .

2017 In the UEFA Euros England stomped through the group stages to face France in the quarter-finals, who they beat 1–0 in an exciting game. They went into the semi-finals with hope and expectation. Could this be another opportunity to reach the Euro final? Sadly, it wasn't, and England were beaten 3–0 by the Netherlands. The team had young and talented players. The Lionesses had to keep believing.

2017 The Women's Super League switched from a summer to a winter calendar, just like men's football. This gave the women a much better chance of success at major tournaments.

2019 The Lionesses won the SheBelieves Cup in America and then went on to the FIFA Women's World Cup in France. It was an exciting tournament and the team went in all guns blazing, once again winning through their group stages. They then beat Norway 3–0 in the quarter-finals. Their semi-final against the USA attracted a new record: 11.7 million viewers on BBC One! England were beaten 2–1 by the fearsome American side, but after the play-offs for third place, they achieved the bronze medal. The Lionesses ended an amazing year by attracting 77,786 fans to Wembley Stadium for their game against Germany. Although they were beaten 2–1, there was much to be happy about. It had been a hugely successful year for the team, with lots of press attention and a record crowd for an England women's match. The Dick, Kerr Ladies with their record match attendance in 1920 would've been proud!

2021 The Netherlands coach Sarina Wiegman took over the Lionesses, keen to help them secure a medal and increase their glory. It was estimated that over 3 million girls and women were taking part in football now, and that number was expected to grow quickly.

2022 England won the Arnold Clark Cup, where invited top teams are challenged to compete against one another. This was their first-ever time winning the title and was achieved after beating other top FIFA countries such as Germany, Spain and Canada.

That wasn't all. The Lionesses were hosting the European Championship in England and they had never looked so good. After easily winning their group stages, they went on to beat Spain 2-1 in the quarter-finals, and then they put on a stunning performance to beat Sweden 4-0. They got through to the final conceding only one goal in the entire tournament. The final was against Germany, their arch-rivals, and in a tense game they won 2-1, with Chloe Kelly scoring the winner in extra-time.

THE LIONESSES WERE NOW
CHAMPIONS OF EUROPE
AND AT THE TOP OF THEIR GAME.

SO LET'S HEAR IT FOR OUR
LIONESSES – PAST AND PRESENT –
I WANT TO HEAR YOU ALL ROAR!

'FIFA say that there are 29 million women and girls now playing football worldwide – isn't that amazing?!'

'That really is a huge number and I guess it's only going to grow?'

'That's the plan! The aim is to get that number up to 60 million by 2026.'

'Well, you heard it here first, readers. Grab those boots and get some practice in!'

'I'm already tying my boots.'

CHAPTER FOUR
REFS, RULES AND MAGNIFICENT MANAGERS

Running up and down the pitch and sidelines are people who might not get as much attention as the players and managers but are a key part of the game – the referees. Their job is to make sure fair play, sportsmanship and rules are followed throughout the game. They can also receive a bit of flack, having to make tricky decisions on the spot, and they work under a lot of pressure, so you can imagine it must be a difficult job at times.

WHAT IS A REFEREE?

A referee is there to make sure that the laws of the game are being followed and that any match is played fairly and safely. It's a very important role. To be a referee in England you must be over fourteen years old, live in the country and complete a referee course with your local County FA so that you are qualified to do the job.

Referees are not alone and have assistant referees working alongside them to support them during the game. Assistant referees will often decide whether someone is offside and which team might be entitled to a throw-in/corner/goal kick. They could be involved in decisions that the referee might have missed, for example, if a player needs to be disciplined or receive medical attention.

To be a good referee or assistant referee you would need to have a good understanding of football, be physically fit and be very calm under pressure.

Most referees working in the WSL and FA Cup are male and it's hoped that more females will be trained in this role.

Does this sound like something you could do?

Could you be the next top referee in the WSL?

SO HOW LONG HAVE REFEREES BEEN USED IN FOOTBALL?

In historical recordings of early football there's no mention of a referee or official overseeing the game. This is probably because in the early nineteenth century, when men's football was building, it was still considered a gentleman's sport – so any matters on the pitch would be sorted out between the teams. Even in the mid-nineteenth century, when references to referees were being made in match records, they would mainly be used to keep time so everyone knew when the game was finished and they could go home for tea!

In 1893 the first formal referees' society was formed and then as the game became more popular, more societies were set up to make sure the rules were being carried out properly.

By 1904 football had become popular worldwide. This led to the creation of FIFA – an international governing body that meant football rules could be applied globally.

In 1906 the FA joined forces with FIFA and over time more rules were introduced to help improve the game.

At the beginning, male referees took charge of women's games and it has only been in more recent times that women have begun to take on this role.

In 2022 FIFA announced that for the first time, women referees and assistant referees would be used to officiate at the men's World Cup in Qatar.

WHAT'S VAR?

VAR (video assistant referee) has been used in the men's Premier League since the 2019/2020 season and was also used in the women's World Cup in 2019 (but it's not used in the Women's Super League).

VAR can help with tricky decisions like tackles in the penalty area, goals cleared off the line or offside positions. It is expensive and extra staff are needed to look after it – but it's possible a VAR-light system could be rolled out to the WSL. This version would use fewer cameras than VAR and wouldn't provide offside or goal line technology, but it would be good news as it would allow the officials to step in if they saw something in the replay that the referee missed. Hopefully it would help the game to be even fairer.

TOP REFEREES

Running around the pitch holding their cards, flags and whistles – who are some of the referees that make the all-important decisions?

AMY FEARN

In February 2010 Amy Fearn became the first woman to referee an English Football League match when she took over the last 20 minutes of a match between Coventry City and Nottingham Forest. This was a huge step as no woman had been appointed as primary officiator before!

SIAN MASSEY-ELLIS

Sian Massey-Ellis has been a match official for over 10 years and juggles being a mum with her challenging referee job. She also got herself into the history books by being the first English female referee in charge of a men's European fixture. Massey-Ellis loves her job and she is keen for more girls and women to consider refereeing.

SALIMA MUKANSANGA

Rwandan referee Salima Mukansanga was the first woman to officiate at the men's edition of the African Cup of Nations. She also officiated at the U-17 Women's World Cup in 2018 and was an official at the 2019 FIFA Women's World Cup in France. Mukansanga has been named as one of the officials in the 2022 men's World Cup in Qatar, making history as one of the first female referees to do so!

KATERYNA MONZUL

Kateryna Monzul was the referee for the Euro 2022 final match, England vs Germany. She had to operate in a sold-out Wembley under lots of pressure and expectation. Only months before the match, Monzul, who is Ukrainian, had been hiding in her hometown of Kharkiv while Russia rained bombs on her country. Monzul was able to flee with her sisters through Moldovia, Hungary, Slovakia, the Czech Republic and Germany before settling in Italy where she resumed her refereeing career.

REBECCA WELCH

Rebecca Welch was a former football player who began refereeing later in her career. Now she is one of the country's leading officials, having overseen the women's FA Cup finals in 2017 and 2020 and also becoming the first woman to taking charge of the men's FA Cup third round. After her regular appearances in the Women's Super League, Welch was promoted to the UEFA elite list of referees and was part of the 2022 Euro campaign.

REFEREE!

What do farting and accidental goals have to do with referees?! See if you already know about these big moments in the world of football refereeing:

- Before 1912, it was legal for a goalkeeper to handle the ball outside the area.

- The average footballer runs around 10 kilometres in a match, and while midfielders have a higher average, even goalkeepers manage around 4.3

kilometres in a game. An assistant referee will run around 9-12 kilometres keeping up with the players.

- In 2018 referee David McNamara resorted to using rock, paper, scissors to settle who kicked off a game because he'd left his coin in the changing room! The FA were not pleased though, because a coin toss is the correct procedure. McNamara received a 21-day ban for not acting in the best interests of the game.

- In England there were 2,146 female referees registered in 2020, which was a 72% increase from 2016.

- Possibly one of the weirdest reasons for being given the red card? Farting! This happened in a Swedish men's game when defender Linden Ljungkvist was playing a game between Järna SK's reserves and Pershagens SK. He was given a red card by referee Dany Kako for showing 'unsportsmanlike behaviour'.

- In 2009 during the World Cup match between England and Cameroon, VAR played a part in overruling an offside decision on a goal. Cameroon appeared to protest this decision and refused to play for several minutes before the end of half-time.

- Can a referee score a goal? Well, in theory, yes. If the ball hit them and bounced into the net, it would count as an indirect goal. However, the referee couldn't decide to suddenly take a shot and go for goal glory themselves!

- Referees will always carry with them the standard equipment: whistle, watch, red and yellow cards, and notebook and pen for recording the match. Referees are not allowed to wear any jewellery and they cannot have a camera on them. So if you spot either of those, you are allowed to show them the red card!

'Did you know that in 1930 a decision was made to look into the rules of football. A man called Stanley Rous was given the job and he worked on these throughout the 1930s.'

'Really? What did he do?'

'He changed the offside rule, meaning an attacking player would be considered onside if he was in line with the next to last defender. He also introduced the back pass rule, meaning a goalkeeper was not allowed to use their hands when a ball was played back to them by a teammate, and the red card was introduced for any tackle from behind.'

'Sounds like he did a good job.'

'He did. No further changes to the rules were made until 1997 and Rous was made President of FIFA in 1961.'

STANDING ON THE SIDELINES

Now let's meet the people standing on the sidelines, the influential coaches behind the English women's football team. These are the people who get to choose which players to use and in what position, will plan strategy and tactics, and instruct their players on the pitch. Good coaches will also motivate and inspire their team and know how to bring the best out of each and every player.

So who have been the key coaches behind the English women's team? Let's go right back to the beginning . . .

Harry Batt (coached from 1969 to 1971)

Harry Batt is seen as the first ever unofficial manager, at a time when women's football was nearly at the end of its ban in England. By all accounts, Batt was a very interesting and intelligent man. He worked as a bus driver and he also spoke five languages. He absolutely loved football and during the FA ban he wanted to know why women couldn't play the game the same as the men did. To him it didn't seem fair at all.

So he decided it was time he started his own team. His team was called the Chiltern Valley Ladies and they were based in Luton. Their first match wasn't a huge success – they lost 12-0 – but it was no matter because they rapidly improved, and soon more talented women wanted to sign with them.

Before long Batt was working with Patricia Gregory – do you remember her from earlier in the book? She was the football fan who wrote angry letters to her newspaper, and in 1969 they both became part of the first governing body, later known as the Women's Football Association (WFA).

However, Batt had bigger plans for women's football – he wanted to create opportunities for them abroad, so he set about creating an English side. This angered the WFA as they had their *own* plans for creating a national team.

Batt began searching the country for the few women's football teams that were still playing at the time, which sadly wasn't many. He travelled across Yorkshire, Lincoln and as far away as Cornwall, and finally he was able to find fifteen women who were keen to play in the unofficial 1971 World Cup in Mexico. This tournament had been arranged by the Fédération Internationale et Européenne de Football Féminin (FIEFF) and had built up huge support and following in Mexico, even if other countries, such as England, weren't as enthusiastic.

Batt had many critics and lots of people laughed at him, wondering why he was bothering to spend so much of his time with this inexperienced team. But Batt had belief. He really believed an English football team could do well. The next problem was that the FA wouldn't support an English women's team in the World Cup, so Batt had to find a sponsor to fund it.

After all his planning and perseverance, sadly - and possibly because the team were used to playing on mucky, dug-up fields instead of professional pitches, and they hadn't the time to train as a team - the women didn't make it past the group stages. The team loved the experience and were overwhelmed by the support

they received overseas, but unfortunately trouble
was waiting for them when they returned home . . .

You Wouldn't Believe It

YWBI

'Here we are, and England's women's team have just returned from Mexico after their 1971 World Cup performance. They've had a great reaction overseas but it looks like they won't be getting quite the same reception here . . .'

'It's definitely looking dicey - the entire team have just been given a six-month ban for breaking the FA rules by attending the World Cup!'

'Unbelievable! And what about their manager, Batt?'

'Well, it's looking even worse for him . . . he's been given a lifetime ban. After all his work to get the tour going, he's said to be heartbroken by the decision.'

Martin Reagan (coached from 1979 to 1990)

Martin Reagan was one of the longest serving coaches of the England women's side for a total of 11 years. Reagan was also an ex-professional player for clubs such as Middlesbrough and York City. He was the manager who gave future head coach Hope Powell her first international game against the Republic of Ireland in 1983. Reagan also managed England to the final of the 1984 European Competition, where they lost to Sweden after a penalty shoot-out. He helped the team to win the Mundialito (known as the little World Cup) twice in 1985 and 1988. Sadly, he was unable to get his team to qualify for the following World Cup and his long period as manager ended. However, Hope Powell would go on to be a future national coach.

'Martin was a real gentleman and a lovely human being [. . .] He was well regarded and well respected by the players. As a coach, he was far more knowledgeable than most of us in the squad had experienced before.'
- Hope Powell

Hope Powell (coached from 1998 to 2013)

In 1998 Hope Powell became the first-ever full-time national coach of the England women's team. This was a huge step, as not only was she the youngest ever England coach, but she was also the first-ever female England coach.

Powell was a talented player herself and scored many goals in her position as attacking midfielder. She played for Millwall Lionesses and then moved on briefly to arch-rivals Friends of Fulham but was soon drawn back to her original club at Millwall. There she became their highest goal-scorer. She helped to set up Bromley Borough, which later merged with Croydon. Powell was involved in four FA Cup finals and in 1996 proudly captained Croydon to a league and cup double. Alongside this, Powell achieved 66 caps for England between 1983 and 1998, scoring 35 goals and was one of six Croydon players who represented England at the FIFA Women's World Cup in 1995.

Keen to progress her career further, Powell began her coaching qualifications aged only nineteen. She would become the first woman to achieve the highest of coaching awards: the UEFA Pro Licence. Just two years later she managed England to the quarter-finals of the European Championship and in 2009 she led them to the European final.

During her 15 years as a manager, Powell led the England team to two World Cup tournaments and four European Championships. In 2013 the England team failed to make it past the group stages in a tricky Euro campaign and after 15 years, Powell's time as head coach ended. Bristol Academy manager Mark Sampson was appointed as the new England boss with former Three Lions striker Marieanne Spacey as his assistant.

Powell is seen by many as a clever and inspiring manager, who was a great mentor to the many players she managed and developed. She helped women's football get noticed and taken seriously in the UK for the first time in many, many years. Powell also helped to push the

English team up the world ranking. She's a footballing force and was awarded both an OBE and a CBE for her contribution to women's football. Hope Powell is seen by many as the creator of the new breed of Lionesses and as the manager who helped pave the way for an ambitious, strong and talented team.

> '*She is a tremendous ambassador for women's football and has been instrumental in the growth of the game.*'
> *- Alex Horne (FA General Secretary, 2013)*

Phil Neville (coached from 2018 to 2021)

Ex-Manchester United defender Phil Neville was appointed as England Women's head coach in 2018. He took over the team when they were in a strong position, third in the FIFA world rankings and a top European side. So much excitement was buzzing about the team.

After winning his first match in charge against France (4-1) in the SheBelieves Cup in 2018, he then helped the team lift the cup for the first time ever in 2019. After wins against Brazil and Japan and a draw with the hosts, the USA, England were crowned SheBelieves winners! Neville also helped the team to qualify for the Tokyo Olympics.

Neville also led the England team in the 2019 World Cup in France. Expectation was particularly high now. The Lionesses were ranked highly. They had an impressive track record. Surely this was the year they could do well?

LET'S GO TEAM!!!

The World Cup ended up being a disappointment, despite the team reaching the semi-finals. It seemed the Lionesses didn't show their true potential and were beaten by a strong USA team, and then were unable to win third place after a disappointing loss against Sweden. The Lionesses also dropped from third place in the world rankings to sixth.

Neville was expected to stay with the team and lead them in their Olympic campaign, but he decided to leave a few months earlier than expected. Neville is now head coach for American club Inter Miami and is a co-owner of Salford City, along with a few of his Manchester United teammates.

Hege Riise (coached in 2021)

Hege Riise will be always known as the coach who led Team GB at the Tokyo Olympics in 2021 and the interim coach who stepped in after Phil Neville left.

Riise is also known as one of the finest players of her generation, and one of Norway's greatest ever players. She won the European Championship, the World Cup and an Olympic gold medal with Norway between 1993 and 2000, and she achieved 188 caps and 58 goals for her country, as well as 1995 Player of the Year.

In the Olympics, Team GB were able to show some impressive football but were beaten in the quarter-finals 4–3 against Australia in a tough match.

However, a new permanent manager was waiting in the wings – ready to help Hege Riise take the Lionesses even further . . .

Sarina Wiegman (coach from 2021 to present)

Sarina Wiegman took over the head coach role for England in 2021 and was considered a very exciting prospect for the team.

Wiegman had already achieved huge success in the Netherlands - leading her team to a UEFA European Championship victory in 2017, being named Best FIFA Women's Coach that same year and then going on to lead the Netherlands to the finals of the World Cup in 2019. Wiegman was a former midfielder who achieved 104 caps for the Netherlands and became the first female player to make 100 appearances. She also captained her side as an international player.

In 2016 Wiegman became the first woman to coach with a men's professional club in the Netherlands, after acting as assistant coach for Sparta Rotterdam. She was a strong and successful coach, leading them to win a league and cup double in 2012.

In 2014 she was called to be the assistant coach with the Dutch women's national team, who just a year later reached the quarter-finals of the World Cup in Canada. Then in 2017 she was finally given the role of head coach on a permanent basis. This would be the beginning of an amazing few years that would see Wiegman's reputation grow and grow. When she took over the lead role at England, expectation was high, but there was also a little fear too. Could Wiegman be the manager who could help the Lionesses secure the major win they so rightly deserved?

And could she help them do it in England?

Well, it seemed the answer was a big fat YES! Sarina Wiegman will be forever remembered in English football history as the first coach to lead the Lionesses to a major title on home soil – and as the manager who put the roar back into the Lionesses' bellies!

CHAPTER FIVE
GAMECHANGERS

Let's look at the goal-scoring, crowd-pleasing Euro 2022 team - from the star team members who played to the talented teammates on the bench. How many players do you already know?

MARY EARPS

Is Mary Earps the beating heart of the Lionesses? You would struggle to find a more committed and passionate player. Not only is she a safe pair of hands in goal, but she's also often the loudest voice on the pitch, encouraging her team to be their best.

Earps started playing football at around eight years old, encouraged by her dad and older brother, who were often kicking a ball around their back garden. Growing up, Earps was frustrated that not many girls played football in parks or at school, so she was happy to practise with her family. Earps loved sports and also took part in dancing, badminton, judo and swimming, but football was her true love and it gave her confidence.

> **'Football really helped me at school.'**
> **– Mary Earps**

By fourteen Earps was playing for Leicester City. She had a trial for Derby but didn't get through – and this wouldn't be the last time her determination was tested. But this is a player who would never give up!

Two years later, Earps moved to Nottingham Forest in the Premier League and then to Doncaster Rovers Belles, where she ended up being their number one keeper. Since then, Earps has played for lots of major teams including Coventry City, Birmingham City, Bristol City, Reading and Vfl Wolfsburg in Germany. In 2019 Earps signed for Manchester United, where she still plays today.

Earps has represented England in under-17, under-19 and under-23 national teams. In 2019 she was named in the FIFA Women's World Cup squad. The Lionesses fought hard and finished fourth, and Earps's place as a reliable and intelligent goalkeeper was secure. During the recent 2022 European Championship, Earps was a key part of England's winning performance, saving shot after shot in the tournament and continuing to cheer her teammates on.

Surely Mary Earps is the roar behind the Lionesses?

Facts & Stats

MARY EARPS

- **Born:** 1993
- **Position:** Goalkeeper
- **Club(s):** Leicester City, Nottingham Forest, Coventry City, Birmingham City, Bristol City, Reading, Doncaster Rovers Belles, Vfl Wolfsburg, Manchester United, England
- **Senior Caps:** 26
- **Senior Clean Sheets:** 19
- **Super Skill:** Flexibility
- **Fantastic Fact:** Earps was dealt a blow when she was dropped by the previous England manager, Phil Neville. She said the decision made her question whether it was the end of her international career, but it became another example of Earps not giving up . . . She continued to believe in herself and ended up playing a huge part in the Euro 2022 tournament.

ELLIE ROEBUCK

One of England's three selected goalkeepers, Ellie Roebuck is a skilled shot-stopper and exciting player with bags of potential and a focused mentality to match.

A true Yorkshire lass, Roebuck grew up a committed Sheffield United fan and was a season ticket holder from a young age. Roebuck used to play at school for fun and was amazed when she got her first England youth call-up.

Roebuck had a great season at Manchester City in 2018, showing off her super goalkeeping skills by making an amazing save against Chelsea. She soon came to the attention of England manager Phil Neville and trained with the SheBelieves team in the USA in 2018, then she made her debut in England's 3-0 victory in Vienna after coming on for Mary Earps.

Roebuck was called up as part of the winning Euro 2022 side and has continued to excel at both club and country level. She is one to watch.

Facts & Stats

ELLIE ROEBUCK

- Born: 1999
- Position: Goalkeeper
- Club(s): Manchester City, England
- Senior Caps: 9
- Senior Clean Sheets: 5
- Super Skill: Composure
- Fantastic Fact: When Roebuck was playing youth football, she played goalkeeper for a boys' side. Most of the boys she played with knew her from primary school and were friends with her already. However, when opposing teams showed up, they would see a girl in goal and think they had the game wrapped up. Roebuck enjoyed showing them they were wrong!

HANNAH HAMPTON

Hannah Hampton was born in Birmingham but spent five years of her childhood in Spain. It was in Spain that she found her passion for football and was soon playing for academy side Villarreal. In 2010 her family returned to England and she joined Stoke City before later signing with Birmingham City in 2016.

In 2013, aged just twelve, Hampton was already representing England in the under-15 squad and went on to pick up caps at under-17, under-19 and under-21 level. Hampton was first brought into the England senior team in March 2020 for the SheBelieves tournament in the USA. In 2022 Hampton made her senior England debut against Spain in the Arnold Clark Cup campaign. She kept a clean sheet in the Lionesses' 0-0 draw and did the same again in their 10-0 victory over North Macedonia. What an amazing record! Hampton is clearly a safe pair of hands and another young goalkeeper to watch out for.

Facts & Stats

HANNAH HAMPTON

- **Born:** 2000
- **Position:** Goalkeeper
- **Club(s):** Villarreal, Stoke City, Birmingham City, Aston Villa, England
- **Senior Caps:** 2
- **Senior Clean Sheets:** 2
- **Super Skill:** Shot-stopping
- **Fantastic Fact:** Hampton initially started out as a striker when she was signed to a Spanish academy team. She only made the switch to keeper when she returned to England in 2010.

LUCY BRONZE

As a young girl, Lucy Bronze enjoyed playing football with her older brother and trying to outskill him (who doesn't like to try and beat their brother or sister?!). She joined her brother's football team, but when she turned eleven Bronze was forced to leave the side because FA rules at the time meant that girls and boys could not play in the same team past this age.

This didn't stop our defender though, and despite an hour's travel each way, Bronze began training at Sunderland's academy alongside other future England stars like Demi Stokes. Going to the academy really helped Bronze develop her football but also her confidence.

More travelling would come as Bronze gained a university scholarship to play for the Tar Heels in North Carolina. She then returned to England to play first at Sunderland and then at Everton, where she worked part time in a pizza shop to support herself. Bronze was also now representing England in the under-19 side.

Bronze hasn't had the easiest journey. She has been hit by two serious knee injuries, one of which nearly stopped her playing for England for good. Bronze fought hard to get herself back to full fitness. It clearly paid off as she made her senior debut for England in 2013 and was included in the team for the Euros in Sweden that year.

She was a key player in the 2015 World Cup, scoring a winner against the hosts, Canada, in the quarter-finals. She was also an instrumental player in the Lionesses' amazing Euro 2022 performance.

Bronze has been voted FIFA Women's Player of the Year 2020 and has won both the Women's Super League and Women's Champions League three times. She is a modest, hardworking and committed player, and many think that she is one of the best players in women's footballing history. What an inspiration!

Facts & Stats

LUCY BRONZE

- Born: 1991
- Position: Defender
- Club(s): Sunderland, Everton, Liverpool, Manchester City, Lyon, Barcelona, England
- Senior Goals: 11
- Senior Caps: 98
- Super Skill: Intensity
- Fantastic Fact: Lucy Bronze's full name is actually Lucia Roberta Tough Bronze and she certainly lives up to the 'tough' part, being one of the most gifted and strong defenders in the country.

JESS CARTER

Jess Carter has dual nationality because her dad is American, but luckily for us she chose to play for England rather than the USA! She was also a talented rugby player and played for Worcester Warriors when she was younger.

Carter became a graduate of Birmingham City's academy and made her debut for Birmingham City against Arsenal aged just sixteen. She is a super versatile player and can play in both midfield and defence. Soon she was representing England at under-19, under-20 and under-21 levels.

Carter played her first senior game for England during the qualifying stages of the 2019 World Cup and soon grabbed everyone's attention by scoring headers against France and Kazakhstan in 2017. Carter had to learn to be patient though, because her next England call-up wouldn't be until four years later under new head coach Wiegman. Carter now plays for Chelsea, where she is a formidable force in defence and another young star waiting to break through the wings.

Facts & Stats

JESS CARTER

- Born: 1997
- Position: Defender
- Club(s): Birmingham City, Chelsea, England
- Senior Goals: 1
- Senior Caps: 12
- Super Skill: Versatility
- Fantastic Fact: In Euro 2022 Carter had the added pressure of facing her partner, German goalkeeper Ann-Katrin Berger, in the final.

ALEX GREENWOOD

Alex Greenwood is a naturally talented player able to play at both central defence and left-back. She is also an expert set piece taker! She joined Everton's academy aged just eight and went on to play for arch-rival teams Manchester United and Manchester City, and Liverpool and Everton (something only former England player Peter Beardsley had achieved before!) She is now an established member of the Manchester City squad after returning from a spell playing in France.

Greenwood gained the achievement of being the youngest member of the 2015 World Cup squad and since then has been a regular fixture in the Lionesses' side. Greenwood is a key part of the Lionesses' defence, and she is also a calm and experienced teammate who is able to motivate others. She dreams of one day captaining the team.

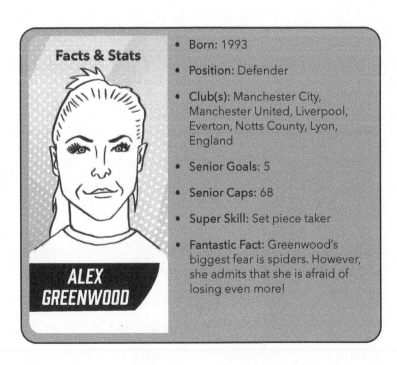

Facts & Stats

ALEX GREENWOOD

- Born: 1993
- Position: Defender
- Club(s): Manchester City, Manchester United, Liverpool, Everton, Notts County, Lyon, England
- Senior Goals: 5
- Senior Caps: 68
- Super Skill: Set piece taker
- Fantastic Fact: Greenwood's biggest fear is spiders. However, she admits that she is afraid of losing even more!

DEMI STOKES

Demi Stokes is a fearless defender who is tough in the tackle and is often regarded as one of the strongest players in the team. Stokes was born in the Midlands but then moved to South Shields, where she would join Sunderland aged sixteen. In 2009 she helped the team reach the FA Cup final. That same year she was part the under-19 England team who won the Euros.

Stokes then received a scholarship to study at the University of South Florida and had her first England call-up while she was in her final year there. Stokes suffered a small blip when she was dropped for the World Cup in Canada in 2015, but she didn't give up and was soon selected once again for the Euro 2017 campaign. She has since been a regular squad member. On the domestic front, Stokes returned to Manchester City in 2015 and has won seven major trophies with them.

Stokes was one of the most experienced players on the Euro 2022 campaign and a crucial part of their storm to success.

Facts & Stats

DEMI STOKES

- Born: 1991
- Position: Defender
- Club(s): Sunderland, Manchester City, England
- Senior Goals: 1
- Senior Caps: 68
- Super Skill: Fearless
- Fantastic Fact: Demi Stokes's hero growing up was former Lioness and all-round legend Rachel Yankey.

LEAH WILLIAMSON

Leah Williamson secured the position of England captain in 2022, taking over from the super talented Steph Houghton. She is happy playing in defence or defensive midfield. She is known for her composure, calm presence and intelligent play. She is the engine room of the team.

She is a huge Arsenal fan and as a young girl used to attend games with her nan. She signed for the team aged only nine and still plays for them now – talk about

dreams coming true! She has won the Women's Super League title with her team as well as the FA Cup.

Williamson has played for her country at every age group from the under-15s to the senior side. She was named England's Young Player of the Year in 2014 after her outstanding performances on the pitch, and she has also won the SheBelieves Cup and Arnold Clark Cup with England.

Williamson was a much-needed presence in the Euro 2022 campaign and in particular formed a strong defensive partnership with teammate Millie Bright. Perhaps Williamson's most poignant moment was making history in the Euro 2022 finals. As captain she got to lift a major trophy for the first time and so became the first Lioness woman ever to do so!

Facts & Stats

LEAH
WILLIAMSON

- Born: 1997

- Position: Defender

- Club(s): Arsenal, England

- Senior Goals: 2

- Senior Caps: 39

- Super Skill: Intelligent play

- Fantastic Fact: Williamson is not just amazing on the pitch; she's dedicated off the pitch too and in her spare time she is studying accountancy.

MILLIE BRIGHT

Millie Bright is a strong and fearless defender. She is also great at last-minute clearances and winning balls in the air. She is definitely a player you want in your last line of defence.

Bright started her domestic career at Doncaster Rovers Belles before moving to Chelsea in 2015. There is no doubt that she has achieved great success by winning the Women's Super League four times, winning the FA Cup three times and reaching the final of the UEFA Champions League in 2021.

Internationally, Bright was a key member of the Euro 2017 campaign and ended up starting every match. She has also shown her skills as goal-scorer, becoming joint top goal-scorer in the Arnold Clark Cup in 2022. Impressive!

Bright brought experience, reliability, skill and technique to the Euro 2022 games, and she had a rock-solid partnership at the back with teammate Leah Williamson.

Facts & Stats

MILLIE BRIGHT

- Born: 1993
- Position: Defender
- Club(s): Doncaster Rovers Belles, Chelsea, England
- Senior Goals: 5
- Senior Caps: 68
- Super Skill: Aerial ability
- Fantastic Fact: Bright suffered with really bad asthma and whooping cough as a child, but luckily these conditions did not hold her back from her professional sporting career.

LOTTE WUBBEN-MOY

Lotte Wubben-Moy is another player with dual nationality, as her father is from the Netherlands. She is a natural defender who is always calm under pressure and able to read the game. She has risen through the ranks of the young Lionesses and has often been selected as captain for them. Wubben-Moy can also be played in defensive midfield.

Another huge Arsenal fan, Wubben-Moy is now lucky enough to play for them, having risen through their ranks as a young girl. Wubben-Moy spent two years playing in the USA but returned to Arsenal in her third year during the COVID-19 outbreak.

Wubben-Moy is a cool and collected player who always looks comfortable with the ball at her feet. She was dealt a blow early in the Euro 2022 campaign when she caught COVID-19 and had to isolate for a week, but she rejoined the squad after the group stages.

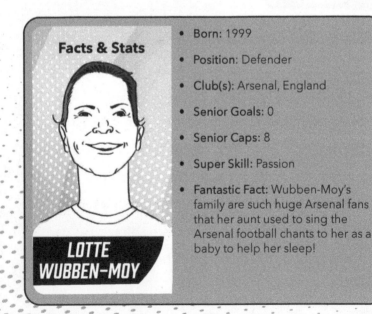

Facts & Stats

LOTTE
WUBBEN-MOY

- Born: 1999
- Position: Defender
- Club(s): Arsenal, England
- Senior Goals: 0
- Senior Caps: 8
- Super Skill: Passion
- Fantastic Fact: Wubben-Moy's family are such huge Arsenal fans that her aunt used to sing the Arsenal football chants to her as a baby to help her sleep!

RACHEL DALY

Rachel Daly is probably the most versatile player in the team: she can be used across the pitch and even as a striker, but most recently has been played as full-back for England. Daly is known for making deadly runs from deep in defence.

Daly was born in Harrogate but has played for American side Houston Dash since 2016. She is the club's record goal-scorer and was voted their most valuable player in 2018. This soon got her noticed and Phil Neville selected her for the SheBelieves Cup that year, for her first appearance in over a year (she scored in her debut match in 2016), and Daly was also named in the 2019 World Cup squad.

Daly is now seen as a key member of Wiegman's defensive line-up and she started all six of England's games in the Euro 2022 tournament. She is also apparently one of the loudest in the changing room!

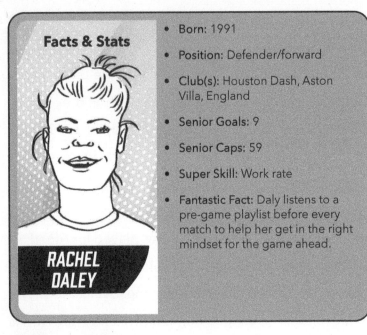

Facts & Stats

RACHEL DALEY

- **Born:** 1991
- **Position:** Defender/forward
- **Club(s):** Houston Dash, Aston Villa, England
- **Senior Goals:** 9
- **Senior Caps:** 59
- **Super Skill:** Work rate
- **Fantastic Fact:** Daly listens to a pre-game playlist before every match to help her get in the right mindset for the game ahead.

KEIRA WALSH

A fantastic defensive midfielder who plays intelligently and dynamically, Keira Walsh is often seen as having one of the best footballing brains. She is able to deliver accurate passes and often opens up play for the Lionesses. She is known to never give up and was coached at eleven years old by Fara Williams.

Walsh captained England aged just twenty-one and is seen as one of the most influential and motivating players on the pitch. She is also a huge Manchester City fan and is proud to play for the club where she has been instrumental in their continuing successes, winning four Continental Cups, three FA Cups and the FA Women's Super League.

Walsh was a huge part of the Euro 2022 winning performance, when her slide pass to Ella Toone set up the opening goal in the final against Germany. She was also named player of the match. What a superstar!

Facts & Stats

KEIRA WALSH

- Born: 1997
- Position: Midfielder
- Club(s): Manchester City, England
- Senior Goals: 0
- Senior Caps: 50
- Super Skill: Intelligent play
- Fantastic Fact: Walsh is such a huge Manchester City fan that she called her pet goldfish Nicolas Anelka and Shaun Goater.

ELLA TOONE

Ella Toone, or 'Tooney', is an expert winger known for weaving her way down the pitch and showing off her skilful moves. She also has an expert eye for a goal!

Toone is a Manchester United fan and started her career in the Manchester United Centre of Excellence before joining Blackburn Rovers and then Manchester City. She returned to Manchester United in 2018 and has gone from strength to strength.

Toone was called into the England squad in 2020 and made her debut in 2021, scoring five times in the first six matches. Under Wiegman she has become a regular member of the team, scoring many goals and even gaining hat-tricks against Latvia and North Macedonia in the World Cup qualifiers.

Facts & Stats

ELLA TOONE

- Born: 1999
- Position: Midfielder/forward
- Club(s): Blackburn Rovers, Manchester City, Manchester United, England
- Senior Goals: 14
- Senior Caps: 23
- Super Skill: Creativity
- Fantastic Fact: Toone won several gymnastics awards when she was younger and was also a talented tennis player.

JILL SCOTT MBE

Jill Scott is a hugely experienced Lionesses and, like Fara Williams, is one of the most capped players of all time. Scott has played for England in four World Cups and four European Championships. In all, she has featured in nine major tournaments and finally lifted the European Championship cup in 2022. What a record!

Scott has also scored key goals in the matches that matter, such as scoring the winner against the Netherlands in the

Euro 2009 semi-finals. Scott can always be relied on to keep a cool head and she's also a key member of the Manchester City team, winning every domestic honour with them. At the end of the 2021/2022 season, Scott was on loan to Aston Villa and ended her contract at Manchester City.

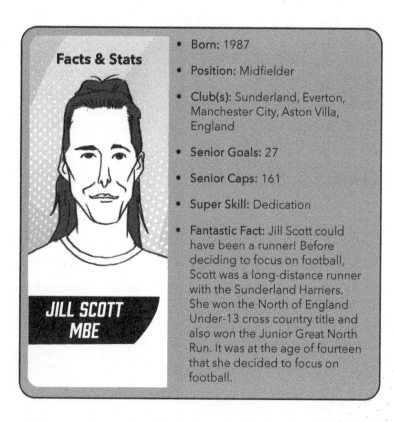

Facts & Stats

- Born: 1987
- Position: Midfielder
- Club(s): Sunderland, Everton, Manchester City, Aston Villa, England
- Senior Goals: 27
- Senior Caps: 161
- Super Skill: Dedication
- Fantastic Fact: Jill Scott could have been a runner! Before deciding to focus on football, Scott was a long-distance runner with the Sunderland Harriers. She won the North of England Under-13 cross country title and also won the Junior Great North Run. It was at the age of fourteen that she decided to focus on football.

JILL SCOTT
MBE

The European Championship in 2022 was the icing on the cake for this gifted and influential player and we know how much it must have meant to her to have been part of the winning side. Scott announced her retirement from football in August 2022 but everyone is excited to see what she does next.

GEORGIA STANWAY

Georgia Stanway is a gifted and powerful midfielder, able to play in centre-forward or wing-back roles. She is also a natural goal-scorer. She grew up with three football-loving brothers who taught her to play. She played with boys until the age of eleven and then was offered to join the girls' youth team at Blackburn Rovers aged thirteen. She remained at Blackburn Rovers until she was sixteen and Manchester City approached her.

Stanway worked her way through the international youth teams, playing in the U-17 World Cup in 2016 and U-20 World Cup in 2018, where the team achieved bronze. She also captained the women's under-19 side to third place in the Euros the same year. She made her senior debut in 2018 against Austria, where she scored! She also went on to help England win the Arnold Clark Cup in 2022.

Stanway started out playing for Manchester City, where she has helped them win several trophies, including the FA Cup in 2019. As of 2022 she announced her move to German side Bayern Munich.

At an international level, Stanway ended up being a major player on the Euro 2022 campaign and one of the stars of the tournament, scoring a winner against Spain in the quarter-finals and starting in all six of the matches.

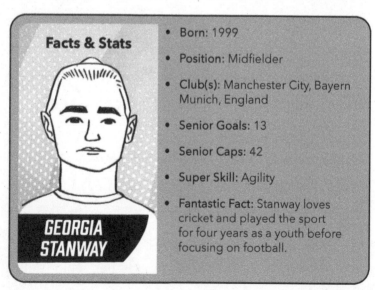

Facts & Stats

GEORGIA STANWAY

- Born: 1999
- Position: Midfielder
- Club(s): Manchester City, Bayern Munich, England
- Senior Goals: 13
- Senior Caps: 42
- Super Skill: Agility
- Fantastic Fact: Stanway loves cricket and played the sport for four years as a youth before focusing on football.

NIKITA PARRIS

Nikita Parris, nickname 'Keets', is a pacey and deadly goal-scorer. Parris was another one of our Lionesses who used to practise her skills with her older brothers, and then she took her football out into the streets of Liverpool where she built her experience even more. Aged seven, she started playing for a local all-boys side until she reached eleven, the age at which girls and boys could no longer play together (at that time).

At fourteen, Parris joined Everton's Centre of Excellence and she soon shot up the ranks, playing for their under-17 side aged just fifteen. Then in 2011 she made the senior team at Everton in the first season of the professional Women's Super League, something Parris had dreamt about as a child. By 2019 Parris was the Women's Super League's all-time top scorer aged only twenty-four. She was named FWA Women's Footballer of the Year in 2019. Parris then played for French club Lyon in 2019, where she was a Champions League winner. After two years abroad, she returned to the UK to play for Arsenal.

In 2016 Parris made her first international appearance for the England women's senior team and scored her first international goal that month. In the 2019 World Cup in France, Parris took a penalty that gave the Lionesses their first win. She ended up being the top scorer in that competition with six goals. She was also part of the England squad that won the SheBelieves Cup in 2019 and the Arnold Clark Cup in 2022, as well as representing Team GB in the Olympics in Tokyo.

Parris made two appearances off the bench in the Euro 2022 campaign and caught the eye of Manchester United, who immediately signed the talented striker.

Facts & Stats

NIKITA PARRIS

- **Born:** 1994
- **Position:** Forward
- **Club(s):** Everton, Lyon, Arsenal, Manchester United, Manchester City, England
- **Senior Goals:** 17
- **Senior Caps:** 69
- **Super Skill:** Shooting
- **Fantastic Fact:** Aged eleven, Parris was frustrated that she could no longer play with the boys in her local team. She was also making waves in her local community and many other girls were inspired to play football just like her. Because of this, Parris helped set up a local women's team that meant she could keep playing for her local area and could also encourage other girls to get involved.

BETH MEAD

Super-striker Beth Mead made her senior debut against Wales in 2018 and is often credited for her powerful shots, lethal right foot and killer crosses.

Born in Whitby, Mead played originally for Middlesbrough (she played for both the local teams, California Boys and California Girls, although both were from Middlesbrough, not California!) before joining Middlesbrough Centre of Excellence aged ten.

At sixteen, Mead joined Sunderland, where she was a standout striker, scoring 77 goals in 78 games. She has since moved to Arsenal, where she is continuing to shine, especially playing wide on the wing. She was voted player of the season in 2021/2022 and scored 14 goals and 19 assists in just 40 club appearances.

Mead has performed well on the international stage and has scored five goals in her first 12 appearances for England since her debut. Mead was disappointed to be left out of the Team GB squad for the Tokyo Olympics, but the arrival of Sarina Wiegman has helped Mead reach new potential. Mead scored 12 goals and contributed towards 12 assists in Wiegman's first 10 games as head coach. Mead was also instrumental in helping England win the Arnold Clark Cup in 2022.

In Euro 2022 Mead started every game and ended up being the competition's top goal-scorer with six goals and five assists, as well as winning the player of the match award twice. She was also named UEFA Player of the Tournament by UEFA's technical observers.

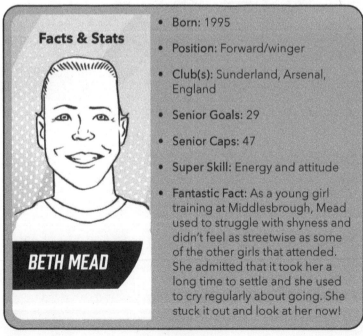

Facts & Stats

BETH MEAD

- Born: 1995
- Position: Forward/winger
- Club(s): Sunderland, Arsenal, England
- Senior Goals: 29
- Senior Caps: 47
- Super Skill: Energy and attitude
- Fantastic Fact: As a young girl training at Middlesbrough, Mead used to struggle with shyness and didn't feel as streetwise as some of the other girls that attended. She admitted that it took her a long time to settle and she used to cry regularly about going. She stuck it out and look at her now!

FRAN KIRBY

Fran Kirby's nickname is 'mini Messi' and its clear to see why. She is an expert at dribbling, passing and moving at speed – and her finishing is top class! It's no wonder she is rated as a player at the top of her game.

Kirby is Chelsea's all-time leading scorer and has helped them to win four Super League titles, three FA Cups and two League Cups.

On the international level, she became the second youngest player when she was selected for the 2015 World Cup and she certainly got herself noticed in the tournament, helping the team to reach third place. Kirby played in all six games of the Euro 2022 tournament, scoring goals against Northern Ireland in the group stages and Sweden in the semi-final.

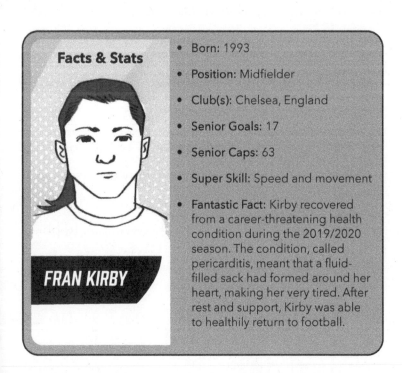

Facts & Stats

FRAN KIRBY

- Born: 1993
- Position: Midfielder
- Club(s): Chelsea, England
- Senior Goals: 17
- Senior Caps: 63
- Super Skill: Speed and movement
- Fantastic Fact: Kirby recovered from a career-threatening health condition during the 2019/2020 season. The condition, called pericarditis, meant that a fluid-filled sack had formed around her heart, making her very tired. After rest and support, Kirby was able to healthily return to football.

ELLEN WHITE

Because there were no girls' football clubs in her area, Ellen White's dad set one up called Mini Dux. This started off an amazing journey for this exceptional striker. White went on to play briefly at Aylesbury Town before being scouted by Arsenal's academy aged only eight.

During her A levels, White left Arsenal to play for Chelsea and became their top scorer three seasons in a row. She then joined Leeds, where after a period of injury she scored twice to help them to the FA Cup in 2010.

White went on to play for Arsenal, where she won seven trophies including three League trophies, and then she played for Notts County, where, in 2015, she played in the first women's FA Cup final to take place in Wembley. She has since moved on to Birmingham City and Manchester City in 2019, where she has continued to be a prolific goal-scorer.

In 2010 White was also called up to play for England for the first time and she scored a goal on her debut! She helped the Lionesses secure third place in the 2015 World Cup in Canada, and in the 2019 World Cup in France she bagged six goals. Her 'goggle eye' celebration has become iconic.

White went on to achieve six goals during the Tokyo 2020 Olympic Games for Great Britain and was part of the attack throughout the Euro 2022 tournament. She scored twice in the six matches she played, is England's all-time top scorer and has been named England Women's Player of the Year three times. In August 2022 White announced her retirement from playing football.

Facts & Stats

ELLEN WHITE

- Born: 1989
- Position: Striker
- Club(s): Arsenal, Chelsea, Leeds, Notts County, Birmingham City, Manchester City, England
- Senior Goals: 52
- Senior Caps: 113
- Super Skill: Composure
- Fantastic Fact: Ellen White's most memorable goal was disallowed! She scored it against the USA in the semi-final of the World Cup in 2019, but VAR disallowed it. It was judged that her toe was in the offside position. If she had been awarded that goal, she would've received the Golden Boot for the most goals scored in the competition, but sadly she finished third behind Megan Rapinoe and Alex Morgan. It also meant that England's dreams were over in the World Cup, as the USA went on to win 2–1. All because of a toe . . .

BETHANY ENGLAND

How apt is Bethany England's surname? Once a young girl playing for a boys' football team, England hoped that one day she would be a future star for her country. She certainly impressed from an early age. She is a skilled finisher and particularly strong in the air, and although she is known for playing upfront, England is also able to play in midfield and wing-back – making her a very useful player!

Born in Barnsley, England started out at Sheffield United's academy before moving on to Doncaster Rovers Belles, where she worked part time at a chip shop to help fund herself. In 2016 she signed to Chelsea, and in 2017/2018 she was loaned to Liverpool, which ended up being a good move as she ended the season as the third highest scorer in the league. Since returning to Chelsea, England has been on great form, helping them to win three Women's Super League titles, three FA Cups and a Continental Cup. She also won the PFA Women's Players' Player of the Year award at Chelsea for the 2019/2020 season.

Internationally, England played at under-19 and under-23 level and played her first senior game in 2019. She was named in Phil Neville's squad for the SheBelieves Cup in 2020 and was called up for Euro 2022, which was her first major tournament. She was part of the squad that won the Euro 2022 trophy and is definitely a player to watch!

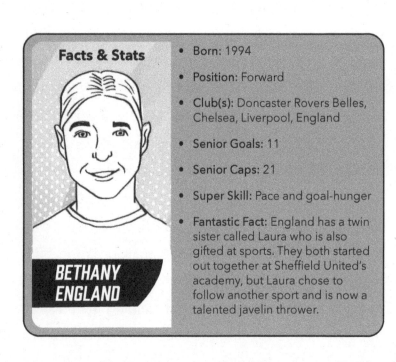

Facts & Stats

BETHANY ENGLAND

- **Born:** 1994
- **Position:** Forward
- **Club(s):** Doncaster Rovers Belles, Chelsea, Liverpool, England
- **Senior Goals:** 11
- **Senior Caps:** 21
- **Super Skill:** Pace and goal-hunger
- **Fantastic Fact:** England has a twin sister called Laura who is also gifted at sports. They both started out together at Sheffield United's academy, but Laura chose to follow another sport and is now a talented javelin thrower.

LAUREN HEMP

Born in Norfolk, this pacey forward and winger rocketed through the ranks of Norwich FC Academy before moving to Bristol City aged sixteen. Within two seasons, Hemp had moved to Manchester City and was playing in Women's Super League topflight.

Hemp was a regular name in City's line-up and is now one of their top scorers, having bagged 30 goals for the club. In 2019 she was part of the Continental Cup-winning side and then scored a goal in the FA final at Wembley against West Ham.

Hemp made her England debut in 2019 and soon became a regular member of the squad. In 2020 she was named as one of Europe's most promising young players. Hemp has won the PFA Women's Young Player of the Year four times and is seen by many as one of the rising stars in English football. Hemp was a key player in the Euro 2022 tournament and it was her deadly corner that led to Chloe Kelly's winning goal in the final against Germany.

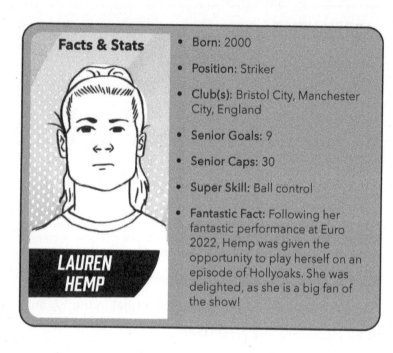

Facts & Stats

LAUREN HEMP

- Born: 2000
- Position: Striker
- Club(s): Bristol City, Manchester City, England
- Senior Goals: 9
- Senior Caps: 30
- Super Skill: Ball control
- Fantastic Fact: Following her fantastic performance at Euro 2022, Hemp was given the opportunity to play herself on an episode of Hollyoaks. She was delighted, as she is a big fan of the show!

CHLOE KELLY

Chloe Kelly is a speedy striker who has already built up a huge following and reputation.

As a child, London-born Kelly was rarely found without a ball at her feet and she credits being the youngest of seven (and having five brothers) as helping her to develop her footballing skills. She often played cage football on the streets of the London estate where she lived. She was spotted by an Arsenal scout and climbed through their academy ranks to make her senior debut aged seventeen in 2015. She went on loan to Everton in 2016 before making a permanent switch there in 2017. In 2020 she moved to Manchester City.

THE WINNING EURO 2022
GOAL CELEBRATION

Kelly played internationally at under-17, under-19 and under-20 level, and she picked up a bronze medal at the FIFA U-20 World Cup in 2018. She was immediately picked out as a rising star of the Lioness team.

Kelly nearly missed the Euro 2022 campaign. She spent a year before it recovering from a knee injury and was lucky to recover in time. But fortunately for us she made it, as she scored the winning goal in extra-time in the final against Germany, securing her role in this historic match and winning legions of fans with her powerful play.

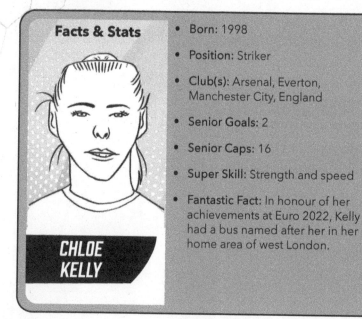

Facts & Stats

- Born: 1998
- Position: Striker
- Club(s): Arsenal, Everton, Manchester City, England
- Senior Goals: 2
- Senior Caps: 16
- Super Skill: Strength and speed
- Fantastic Fact: In honour of her achievements at Euro 2022, Kelly had a bus named after her in her home area of west London.

CHLOE KELLY

ALESSIA RUSSO

Alessia Russo is a domineering and commanding striker with a clinical shot. Born in Kent, Russo first played football at the age of nine for Bearstead United Under 9 boys' team and then for the girls' Under 10 team. She then climbed up the ranks of the Chelsea development teams before moving on to Brighton & Hove Albion in 2017.

Russo studied at college in America while playing for the North Carolina Tar Heels. During this period Russo was part of the young Lionesses team and was in the squad that bought home the bronze medal in 2018 U-20 Women's World Cup. In 2020 Russo returned to England, signing for Manchester United for two years.

Russo has been capped at every age group for England. She started in the senior team in 2020 when she took part in the SheBelieves Cup. In 2021 Russo secured a hat-trick in an impressive 20-0 victory over Latvia. It was the fastest hat-trick scored in the Lionesses' history. How impressive is that!

Russo's back-heel goal (already being nicknamed 'the Russo') in England's semi-final defeat of Sweden in Euro 2022 is seen by many as the best goal in the competition. She made five appearances off the bench and scored 4 goals. Russo is an exciting young member of the team and has already scored an impressive number of goals for her country.

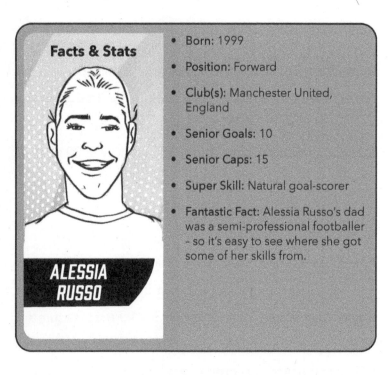

Facts & Stats

- Born: 1999
- Position: Forward
- Club(s): Manchester United, England
- Senior Goals: 10
- Senior Caps: 15
- Super Skill: Natural goal-scorer
- Fantastic Fact: Alessia Russo's dad was a semi-professional footballer – so it's easy to see where she got some of her skills from.

ALESSIA RUSSO

NAMES TO LOOK OUT FOR

A team is bigger than the players on the pitch for a game – so let's meet some of the other Lionesses who were on the fringes of Euro 2022 and are names to watch out for in the future.

Jordan Nobbs

A wonderfully creative midfielder, Jordan Nobbs sadly missed the Euro 2022 selection due to a knee injury. She has been a key member of the Lionesses' in the past, having starred in both Euro 2013 and Euro 2017. Nobbs is also a possible future coaching star and is currently working towards her coaching qualifications.

Sandy MacIver

Sandy MacIver is a talented and highly rated goalkeeper but fell victim to there being too many goalkeeping options for the Euro 2022 campaign. MacIver has represented England at youth levels and won the Golden Glove as the tournament's best keeper at the U-20 World Cup in France. She recently moved to Manchester City in July 2022 and is one to watch.

Lucy Staniforth

Lucy Staniforth is a well-respected attacking midfielder who played in the 2019 World Cup. She made her debut senior appearance in 2018. She was also part of the squad that went on to win the SheBelieves Cup.

Katie Zelem

This Manchester United star is another skilled midfielder and captain who has been making waves in the Women's Super League as a solid central player. She has featured regularly as a young Lioness, playing in under-15s through to under-23s, and was part of the senior squad who won the Arnold Clark Cup in 2022.

Ebony Salmon

Ebony Salmon is an impressive forward. At youth level, Salmon has represented England at under-17, under-19 and under-23 levels and has often been given the captain's armband too. During the U-17 Women's Euros in 2018 she got herself a hat-trick. Salmon remains an exciting young prospect for the Lionesses moving forward.

Niamh Charles

A creative defender Niamh Charles was playing football at the age of just four before signing to Liverpool's academy. She has played for England's under-17 side and has already achieved a few caps for the senior England side. She now plays for Chelsea.

Maya Le Tissier

Maya Le Tissier is a skilful and intelligent defender who captained the under-17 side at the UEFA U-17 Championship and has since played for U19 and U23 Lionesses. Le Tissier joined Manchester United from Brighton & Hove Albion in 2022 and holds the Women's Super League record for the highest number of appearances made as a teenager.

Esme Morgan

Esme Morgan, a defender, has risen through the ranks at Manchester City Academy since the age of fourteen and made her first team appearance shortly after her GCSEs. Morgan's international hopes were put on hold when she broke her leg in 2021, sadly putting her out of action for the 2021/2022 season. However, Morgan signed a three-year contract extension at Manchester City in January 2022 and we should see her back to her best very soon.

Jess Park

Jess Park, a strong striker, has impressed with her natural goal-scoring ability and has represented England at under-17, under-19 and under-23 level, scoring 20 goals in 26 appearances. In 2017 she joined Manchester City and many think she will be a future England star.

Have any of these players inspired you? Who are you looking forward to watching in the future?

Many of these players have faced knockbacks - whether it be through injury, selections or self-doubt - but none of them have given up. These committed players have continued to improve and to be the best that they can be. And with the 2023 Women's World Cup to be played in Australia and New Zealand, we have more exciting games to come!

GO, LIONESSES!

CHAPTER SIX
FOOTBALLING AROUND THE WORLD

Up until now we have focused on England and our Lionesses, but what about the rest of the world? The great news is that women's football really has been hitting the heights worldwide and is growing and growing in popularity. So where else has women's football excelled, which footballers have hit stardom and what mind-boggling football facts can we discover? Let's whizz about the globe for fantastic football facts and meet just a few of the international stars that get the crowds cheering.

Fantastic Fact: A football game is 90 minutes long, right? Well, not in the Women's World Cup in 1991. Only 80 minutes of football was played, and soon after they added the extra 10 minutes to match the men's game.

NORTH AMERICA

Top League: National Women's Soccer League (NWSL).

International Home Kit: White top with red and blue stripes on the sleeves. The World Cup shirt in 2019 (which featured three stars on the back) was Nike's bestselling football shirt of all time during that season.

The USWNT (United States Women's National Team) is one of the best in the world and is often the team to beat in international competitions. They are the most successful World Cup side, having won the trophy four times!

Famous Moments:

- In the 2019 World Cup, US striker Alex Morgan celebrated her goal against England by miming sipping a cup of tea. This was seen by some as a swipe at the English players (and England's love of the drink). However, others have since suggested that Morgan may have been referring to the expression 'sipping tea' as in 'sharing gossip'. Who knows what the truth might be?

- In the 2012 Olympics semi-final match against Canada, Alex Morgan scored a header in the dying seconds of extra-time to take her team into the final – where they would pick up gold.

- In the 2015 World Cup, Carli Lloyd had an amazing game against Japan in the final. She scored a hat-trick, but if that wasn't enough, her incredible third goal was from the halfway line. This goal is often replayed on YouTube as a wonder goal to be remembered!

Fantastic Fact: US national player Mia Hamm could be seen as the first women's international football star - and she's even had her own video game.

Fantastic Fact: In the 1999 Women's World Cup final, over 90,000 fans packed into the stands to watch the USA vs Chile. The match went to penalty shoot-out and the USA's Brandi Chastain secured the winning shot. She whipped off her shirt and ran towards the crowd, making this an iconic moment in American sporting history.

Fantastic Fact: The first women's world cup in 1991 wasn't officially called the 'world cup'. Instead, FIFA named it the 'FIFA Championship for Women's Football for the M&M's Cup'. No surprise it didn't catch on . . .

Top League: Scottish Women's Premier League (SWPL).

International Home Kit: Navy blue.

Fantastic Fact: Speedy midfielder Kim Little is viewed as one of the best Scottish women footballers of all time. Her historic volley against Albania in 2018 was enough to qualify Scotland for their first ever Women's World Cup place. What goal could have been sweeter?!

WALES

Top League: Adran Premier.

International Home Kit: Red.

Fantastic Fact: Jess Fishlock is a skilled midfielder, able to pull off long-range shots and creative runs. She is the first footballer (male or female) to gain 100 caps for Wales.

Fantastic Fact: Wales has seen a boom in girls and women taking up football – by 2021 there had been a 50 per cent rise in playing numbers in the past five years.

CANADA

Top League: Currently there is no women's premier league in Canada - the league is semi-professional and a level below the NSWL in America. Players are campaigning for this to change.

International Home Kit: Red with a subtle maple leaf background.

Famous Moments:

- Canada secured the biggest margin of victory in a World Cup qualifier when they beat Puerto Rico 21-0 in the 1998 CONCACAF W Championship.

- In the Tokyo Olympics, Canada faced their US arch-rivals in the semi-finals. Canada were keen to seek revenge after losing to the same team in the London Olympics in 2012. The only goal was scored from a penalty, Jessie Fleming ensuring she hit the back of the net. Canada ended up winning gold in the final after a tense penalty shoot-out against Sweden.

Fantastic Fact: As of July 2022, powerful forward Christine Sinclair had scored an amazing 190 goals in 314 appearances for her national side.

BRAZIL

Top League: Campeonato Brasileiro de Futebol Feminino Série A1.

International Home Kit: Yellow with green trim.

Famous Moment: Marta scored a famous goal in the 2007 World Cup semi-final against the United States. Her speed left the defender on the back foot and then a brilliant finishing shot past the American keeper helped the Brazilians to a 4-0 victory.

Fantastic Fact: Marta, like Pelé, is known by her first name alone – and she's nicknamed 'Pelé in skirts' because she is regarded as one of the most skilful and notable footballers of all time. As of 2022 she had achieved 17 World Cup goals and six FIFA World Player of the Year awards.

Fantastic Fact: Women's football also suffered a ban in Brazil. From 1941–1979, women were not allowed to play football, and the first league wasn't formed until 1981.

GERMANY

Top League: Frauen-Bundesliga – one of the most established leagues in the world.

International Home Kit: White with subtle black striping and hints of orange on the sleeve.

Famous Moment: When Alexandra Popp scored against France in the semi-finals of the 2022 Euros, it made her the first player ever to score in five successive matches at the women's Euros.

Fantastic Fact: Germany won the 2003 and 2007 World Cups. In the 2007 campaign they beat Argentina 11-0 in their opening match, which at the time was the highest number of goals a team had scored in a women's World Cup match!

Fantastic Fact: In the nineties German forward Heidi Mohr was seen as one of best players of her time. And for good reason. Mohr was an integral player for Germany for over a decade, and in her two World Cup appearances (1991 and 1995) she scored 10 goals in 12 games. She has since been elected into the German Football Hall of Fame.

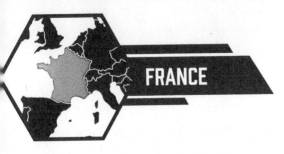

FRANCE

Top League: Division 1 Féminine.

International Home Kit: Blue with an all-over floral motif (to represent French art and architecture). Inside the collar is the slogan 'our differences unite us'.

Famous Moment: Melvine Malard scored the fastest goal of the 2022 Euros by hitting the back of the net in 43 seconds. The game against Iceland ended as a 1-1 draw and the Icelandic team were sent home from the tournament despite being unbeaten.

Fantastic Fact: Kadidiatou Diani is a huge force in the French league, able to play both upfront and midfield. She is one of the highest paid female footballers in the world.

Fantastic Fact: By 2021 Marie-Antoinette Katoto achieved 132 goals in 148 matches!

Fantastic Fact: Goal-scoring defender Wendie Renard headed goals in the 2019 World Cup that made many compare her to Dutch footballing legend Virgil van Dijk.

THE NETHERLANDS

Top League: Vrouwen Eredivisie

International Home Kit: Orange with a black stripe – the Dutch symbol is a lion, and this plus the kit colour gives the team their nickname the Orange Lionesses.

Fantastic Fact: As well as being an incredible player for her national side, Dutch forward Vivianne Miedema is an Arsenal superstar. By 2021 she had scored 100 goals for her club in just 110 games!

Top League: Primera División – the home to many famous footballers!

International Home Kit: Red with navy and yellow trim.

Fantastic Fact: Barcelona legend Alexia Putellas is an international footballing star, having won the Ballon d'Or (the greatest football award in the world) and being named best FIFA women's player. With Barcelona she has won every trophy there is to win!

Top League: A-League Women.

International Home Kit: Gold with a green trim.

Fantastic Fact: Early in 2022, Australia began their Women's Asian Cup campaign against Indonesia and ended up with a record-breaking 18-0 win. Sam Kerr scored five goals, including a hat-trick within the first 27 minutes!

Fantastic Fact: Australian forward Sam Kerr is the highest rated female player on FIFA 19 and her rating of 89 is higher than Mohamed Salah.

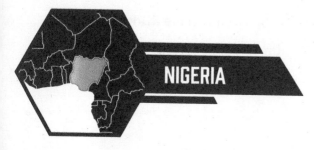

NIGERIA

Top League: NWFL Premiership (formerly the Nigeria Women Premier League).

International Home Kit: White and light green patterned.

Famous Moment: Nigeria put on an entertaining

performance in the 1999 World Cup, where they made it to the quarter-finals. They were praised for their flair and flamboyant play, and player Mercy Akide (Marvellous Mercy) coloured her hair green and white to match the joy of the occasion!

Fantastic Fact: Asisat Oshoala was the first footballer in the world to be named BBC Women's Footballer of the Year in 2015.

SOUTH KOREA

Top League: WK League.

International Home Kit: Pink/red with fade design and black edging.

Fantastic Fact: Ji So-yun is the country's top scorer and one of the most capped players. She has been named

South Korea's Women's Footballer of the Year six times.

Top League: Chinese Super League.

International Home Kit: Red with a yellow trim.

Fantastic Fact: Sun Wen is considered one of the greatest female footballers of all time with a long career that lasted from 1989 until 2006.

There are many, many countries and players that we haven't mentioned. The truth is there are so many amazing international stars out there and so many to be excited about – we'd need another book to include them all! Have you discovered a new international footballing star that you'd like to follow?

CHAPTER SEVEN
TIME TO BE A GAFFER

You've met the Lionesses past and present, the managers and coaches, the referees and some incredible international players. Now it's your turn to design your *own* ultimate women's team.

If you could choose any players from throughout history, who would you include? What will you call your team and why?

- Choose your formation. Are you going to play in 4, 4, 2, or 3, 5, 2 or maybe even 4, 5, 1?

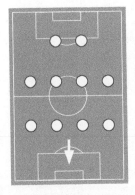 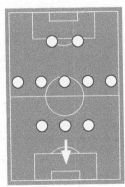 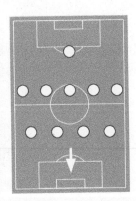

- Choose your goalkeeper

- Choose your defensive backline. Who will you pick? A selection from the current England team? A rising star? Or maybe someone from the past?

- Choose your midfield. Are you playing wingers out wide? Who do you fancy to start up an attack?

- Choose your forwards. Which striker do you want on the pitch? A current regular? A previous record-breaker or an international star?

- Who will be your captain?

- Perhaps you can be part of this amazing new side too. What position will you play? What number will you wear?

Now consider which manager you'd like to run things. Will you be choosing the experienced and patient Powell, the rising talent of Neville, the wonder that is Wiegman or maybe someone else entirely?

Where in the world and on which ground are you going to play your first match? Who will referee?

What kit will your team play in? You can design it! Think about the colour, the badge, and the home and away strips.

And which team are you going to choose to play against? Can you predict the score?

Good luck!

CHAPTER EIGHT
QUIZ TEAMS AT THE READY

Let's see how much you can remember from this crowd-cheering rollercoaster through women's football. Here's your chance to show off how much you now know.

Maybe you can test your family, friends, even your dog?

Are YOU an expert England fan?

1) What was the apt name of the nineteenth-century woman who campaigned to start women's football in England?

2) On what ground did the Dick, Kerr Ladies play in front of a record-breaking crowd of 53,000 in 1920?

3) Which year was the FA ban and how long did it last?

4) What was the name of the Dick, Kerr Ladies striker who scored over 900 goals in her career?

5) Which former England and Arsenal star is now a leading sports presenter and TV personality?

6) Who is considered England's first manager?

7) What year did Hope Powell take over as manager?

8) Alexia Putellas is a legendary player for which country?

9) Who scored the winner for England in extra time against Germany in the Euro 2022 final?

10) Which head coach led England to victory in Euro 2022?

11) Who scored the most goals for England in Euro 2022?

12) Who was England's captain in 2022?

13) Which international player is referred to as 'Pelé in skirts'?

14) Which match in the 1999 World Cup attracted 90,000 fans?

15) Where will the 2023 Women's World Cup be held?

How did you do?

0-3

You might need some extra coaching and warm-up exercises to get you fully up to speed. Give it another go!

4-8

You are currently on the bench and looking like you might get some time to shine on the pitch. Some practice is needed.

9-11

You are a rising superstar and showing great skill and promise. Keep it up!

12-15

Well done! You are a gamechanging superstar and top England fan!

CHAPTER NINE
STOPPAGE TIME

We have now reached the end of our gamechangers journey, and I hope that you have enjoyed it as much I have enjoyed writing it. There really is so much to be proud of, especially when we look at footballing history and see the achievements that women have made over time. I would like to think that the older pioneers like Nettie Honeyball and the Dick, Kerr Ladies would be so happy to see where our Lionesses are now and would be excited to see where they might end up in the future. It is a great time to be a Lioness fan!

The journey has been quite a rollercoaster. We have discovered war-time heroes raising lots of money for charity, record-breaking match crowds, early international matches and football stars from the past who were loved and respected. We have read about the FA ban that rocked the footballing world and the people that followed after. And we've witnessed the rise of women's football against the odds to become the inspirational and top-level game that it is today.

It is the journey that has made success even sweeter today. We know how hard the Lionesses have had to fight and how far they've come. They have taught us that hard work, commitment, self-belief and teamwork really *do* pay off.

So this is my challenge to you now: can you be a future gamechanger? Are you inspired to give football a go, even if it's just for fun? Maybe you can be a future player, manager or referee? The country needs more talented players and you could be one of them. After all, you never know until you try.

If you've been inspired by this book and don't belong to a football club, remember it's never too late to give it a go. You can join most clubs at any age or ability and it's a great way to get fit, make new friends and learn new skills. You can find out about most local grassroots clubs through your school or via the FA website.

Or perhaps, like me, you might not be as sporty, but you can still support the women's game. Go along and watch a game and take your family and friends. Be one of the loudest and happiest supporters. Help future Lionesses to thrive. Watch the games on TV, talk about them at school and home, and wear the shirt with pride.

Because the story doesn't end here . . . The Women's World Cup is just around the corner and yet more competitions such as the Arnold Clark Cup await after that. Who knows how many more trophies and awards our Lionesses can collect? Whatever happens, you'll know from this book that the game will be exciting and worth watching.

So let's go and enjoy the game! And remember, we can all be gamechangers.

Eve x